MASTERING SYSTEM ARCHITECTURE WITH ASSEMBLY AND MACHINE LANGUAGE

From Microarchitecture to Advanced Performance Tuning and Hardware Control

NATHAN WESTWOOD

TABLE OF CONTENTS

ABOUT THE AUTHOR!

Dr. Nathan Westwood

Biography:

Dr. Nathan Westwood is a pioneering technologist known for his exceptional contributions to the fields of software development, cloud computing, and artificial intelligence. With a passion for innovation and a relentless drive to solve complex problems, Nathan has become a prominent figure in the tech industry, shaping the future of digital technology.

Born and raised in Silicon Valley, Nathan's interest in technology started at a young age. His fascination with computers and coding led him to pursue a degree in Computer Science from Stanford University, where he excelled academically and honed his skills in programming and software engineering. During his time at Stanford, Nathan was involved in several cutting-edge projects that sparked his interest in AI and cloud technologies.

After graduating, Nathan joined a leading tech firm where he played a key role in developing cloud-based solutions that revolutionized data storage and analytics. His work in the early stages of cloud computing set the foundation for modern infrastructure-as-a-service (IaaS) platforms, earning him recognition as one of the industry's emerging stars. As a lead engineer, Nathan was instrumental in launching products that have since become industry standards.

Nathan's entrepreneurial spirit led him to co-found his own tech startup focused on AI-driven automation tools for businesses. Under his leadership, the company rapidly gained traction, attracting both investors and clients who were eager to leverage his innovative AI solutions to streamline operations and improve efficiency. Nathan's commitment to pushing the boundaries of what's possible in tech quickly earned him a reputation as a visionary leader.

Known for his expertise in machine learning, Nathan has also worked with several large tech companies, advising on the integration of AI and data science into their operations. His work has spanned various sectors, including healthcare, finance, and manufacturing, where he has helped organizations harness the power of data and automation to achieve exponential growth.

Beyond his technical achievements, Nathan is a sought-after speaker at global tech conferences, where he shares his insights on the future of cloud computing, artificial intelligence, and the ethical challenges posed by emerging technologies. His thought leadership and commitment to ethical innovation have made him a respected voice in the tech community.

In addition to his professional accomplishments, Nathan is deeply passionate about mentoring the next generation of tech leaders. He regularly contributes to educational programs and initiatives designed to inspire young minds and equip them with the skills necessary to thrive in the ever-evolving tech landscape.

Nathan Westwood continues to be a trailblazer in the tech industry, shaping the future of technology with his innovative ideas, entrepreneurial spirit, and commitment to making a positive impact on the world.

Chapter 1: Introduction to System Architecture

OBJECTIVE:

In this chapter, we will explore the essential components and principles that define system architecture. By the end of this chapter, you'll have a solid understanding of how systems are designed, how they communicate internally, and the impact of this communication on real-world applications in various industries. We will also discuss key historical milestones and the evolution of the microprocessor, shedding light on how system architecture has evolved over the decades. Understanding these concepts will not only give you insights into computer engineering but also help you appreciate how modern computing systems work at a deep, fundamental level.

1.1 What is System Architecture?

System architecture refers to the high-level design and organization of a computing system. It defines how all the components of the system interact and work together to perform tasks. These components include the central processing unit (CPU), memory (RAM), input/output devices (I/O), and various other peripherals and storage systems. System architecture also outlines how the hardware components communicate with each other, how data is stored, accessed, and processed, and how the system interacts with software.

At its core, system architecture is about structuring the system in a way that balances efficiency, performance, cost, and flexibility. The design of a computer system's architecture can vary greatly depending on its intended use — whether it's a simple embedded system or a complex high-performance supercomputer.

1.2 How Systems are Designed and How They Communicate

A system's design starts with a clear understanding of its goals. The first step is determining what the system needs to accomplish. Will it be used for general computing tasks? Is it designed for gaming, data processing, or scientific simulations? These goals directly impact the architectural decisions made during the design phase.

Key Components of a System Design:

1. **CPU (Central Processing Unit)**: The CPU is the heart of any system. It processes instructions, handles computations, and manages data flow within the system. The design of the CPU is critical to system performance. Over the years, CPUs have evolved from single-core to multi-core processors, allowing for parallel processing, significantly enhancing performance.
2. **Memory (RAM)**: RAM is where the system stores data that is actively being processed. A fast and efficient memory system allows for quicker access to this data, which speeds up the overall performance of the system. RAM size and speed are critical factors in system performance.
3. **I/O (Input/Output)**: I/O refers to the mechanisms by which the system communicates with the outside world. Input devices like keyboards, mice, and sensors provide data to

the system, while output devices like monitors, printers, and speakers display or act on that data.

4. **Clock Cycle**: The clock cycle determines how quickly the CPU can process instructions. Modern processors use high-frequency clock cycles to process billions of instructions per second.

How These Components Communicate:
The components of a system communicate through a series of buses, pathways that transmit data and control signals between the CPU, memory, and I/O devices. Data is transferred using electrical signals, and each component needs to be able to interpret these signals properly.

A typical communication model is based on the **Von Neumann architecture**, which uses a single memory space for both instructions and data. However, modern systems often use different architectures to improve performance, such as **Harvard architecture**, which separates data and instruction memory.

1.3 Historical Context: The Evolution of Microprocessors and Assembly Programming

To understand system architecture, it's essential to trace its evolution over time. The microprocessor — the heart of modern computing systems — has come a long way since its inception. Understanding its history provides context for how system design has transformed.

1. **The Early Days**:
   The first microprocessor, the **Intel 4004**, was introduced in 1971. It was a groundbreaking development, capable of

executing simple instructions for the first time on a single chip. This 4-bit processor marked the beginning of the shift from large, room-sized computers to compact, efficient systems.

2. **The Rise of 8-bit and 16-bit Processors**:
Following the 4004, Intel released the **Intel 8008** (8-bit processor) and the **Intel 8086** (16-bit processor) in the mid-1970s and early 1980s. These processors began to handle more complex tasks, and with them came advancements in memory and I/O management.

3. **The Transition to 32-bit and 64-bit**:
By the early 1990s, computing power was advancing rapidly, and the introduction of 32-bit and 64-bit processors marked the next era. These processors allowed for greater memory addressing capabilities and faster performance. They also made multitasking and real-time computing possible on personal computers.

4. **The Modern Era and Multi-Core Processors**:
Today, microprocessors are incredibly advanced. **Multi-core processors** (with two or more CPU cores on a single chip) allow for better multitasking and performance. This shift was driven by the limitations of clock speeds — increasing the clock speed alone couldn't continue to improve performance, so processors began to focus on executing multiple instructions simultaneously.

Assembly Language:
In parallel with the evolution of the microprocessor came the development of **assembly language**. In the early days, programming was done using **machine code** — the raw binary instructions that the CPU could directly execute. However, machine code is difficult for humans to understand, so assembly language was developed as a human-readable representation of machine code.

Assembly language allows programmers to write low-level programs with mnemonics that correspond to machine instructions, making the code more understandable. For example, instead of writing a binary sequence to add two numbers, an assembly language programmer could write a simple instruction like `ADD R1, R2`. This advancement made it easier to program and control hardware.

1.4 Real-World Applications: How System Architecture Impacts Industries

Understanding system architecture is essential not just for academic purposes but for practical applications in the real world. Let's explore how system architecture plays a critical role in industries like healthcare, robotics, and gaming.

1. **Healthcare**:
    Modern healthcare systems rely heavily on technology, from patient management software to advanced diagnostic tools. System architecture plays a key role in ensuring that data is processed quickly and accurately. For instance, in **medical imaging**, complex algorithms require high-performance processors to handle large data sets efficiently. Similarly, **telemedicine** systems depend on robust system architectures to handle real-time video calls and medical data transmission.
2. **Robotics**:
    Robots, particularly those used in manufacturing and healthcare, require high-precision, real-time processing of sensor data. The system architecture in a robot includes specialized microcontrollers and memory systems that enable rapid sensor input processing. Assembly programming is often used to directly control the robot's movements and actions, providing the necessary speed and accuracy for operations like robotic surgery or autonomous vehicles.

3. **Gaming**:
   The gaming industry is another area where system architecture is critical. Modern gaming consoles and PC systems need to process graphics, sound, and complex interactions in real-time, often at high frame rates (60 frames per second or higher). Advanced processors, GPUs (Graphics Processing Units), and memory systems are required to handle the immense computational demands of modern games. Understanding system architecture allows game developers to optimize their code for performance, ensuring smooth gameplay and reducing lag.

1.5 Key Terms and Concepts

To fully grasp system architecture, you need to understand some essential terms and concepts that define how computers are structured and operate.

- **CPU (Central Processing Unit)**: The primary processing unit in a computer. It carries out instructions from programs, performs calculations, and manages data flow.
- **RAM (Random Access Memory)**: A type of volatile memory that stores data currently being used or processed by the CPU. It is essential for quick access to active data.
- **I/O (Input/Output)**: The interface between the computer and external devices (like keyboards, monitors, printers). I/O systems manage the exchange of data between the computer and its peripherals.
- **Clock Cycles**: The basic unit of time in a computer, determined by the processor's clock. Each clock cycle represents one step in processing an instruction.
- **Registers**: Small, fast storage locations within the CPU that hold data and instructions currently being processed.

- **Cache**: A small, high-speed memory located inside or near the CPU, used to store frequently accessed data.
- **Bus**: A system of pathways used for communication between components in the computer. The CPU, memory, and peripherals are connected by buses that allow them to transfer data.

Conclusion

In this chapter, we have introduced the fundamental principles of system architecture and its significance in computer engineering. We've discussed how systems are designed, how components communicate, and the importance of assembly language in early computing systems. We also explored how system architecture is vital in real-world applications, from healthcare to gaming and robotics.

As we progress through this book, we will build on these concepts, diving deeper into the specifics of microprocessors, memory systems, and advanced performance tuning. Understanding system architecture is the first step in becoming proficient in low-level programming and hardware design, and it is a key skill for anyone working in the fields of computer engineering, robotics, or any area where performance and efficiency are critical.

Chapter 2: The Fundamentals of Assembly Language

OBJECTIVE:

In this chapter, we will explore the basics of **assembly language**, a low-level programming language that sits between high-level languages (like Python or Java) and machine language (the binary code executed directly by the computer's CPU). Assembly language is essential for anyone looking to understand how software interacts with hardware at the deepest level. By the end of this chapter, you will be able to understand the core components of assembly language, how it operates within a system, and how to write simple assembly programs. This knowledge will set the stage for learning more advanced topics in system architecture and low-level programming.

2.1 What is Assembly Language?

Assembly language is a low-level programming language that provides a symbolic representation of the machine code instructions that a computer's processor can execute directly. Unlike high-level languages, which are abstract and human-readable, assembly language offers a closer, more direct interface with the hardware. It allows programmers to write instructions in a format that is easier to understand than raw binary machine code, yet still very much tied to the architecture of the underlying hardware.

- **Machine Code**: This is the binary code (composed of 0s and 1s) that the CPU understands and executes. It is specific to each type of CPU and varies depending on the hardware architecture.
- **Assembly Language**: Assembly language acts as a human-readable version of machine code. Each instruction in an assembly program corresponds to one or more machine code instructions. However, rather than using binary, assembly uses mnemonic codes, making it easier for programmers to write and understand.

For example:

- A machine code instruction might look like this: `110100101011`
- In assembly language, the same instruction could be represented as `MOV A, B` (which means "move the contents of register B into register A").

The beauty of assembly is that it gives the programmer a way to control the hardware directly, offering fine-grained control over how the computer operates, which is crucial for performance-critical applications.

2.2 The Structure of an Assembly Language Program

An assembly language program is typically made up of a series of instructions that the CPU can execute. These instructions are broken down into components that help the computer understand what needs to be done. A typical assembly program has the following structure:

1. DIRECTIVES

Directives are special commands that provide instructions to the assembler (the tool that converts assembly language code into machine code). Directives tell the assembler how to organize the code, allocate memory, or define constants. They are not executed by the CPU but help in structuring the program.

Example:

asm

```
SECTION .data
```

This directive indicates that the following section will contain data definitions.

2. LABELS

Labels are used to mark specific points in the program. Labels help define the locations in memory where certain data or instructions reside, allowing the program to jump to these locations when necessary (such as during loops or function calls).

Example:

asm

```
start:
    MOV AX, 1
```

In the example above, `start` is a label marking a specific part of the program.

3. INSTRUCTIONS

Instructions are the actual commands that the CPU executes. These instructions are typically mnemonics that correspond to low-level operations such as moving data, performing calculations, or jumping to a different part of the program.

Example:

asm

```
MOV AX, 5       ; Move the value 5 into register AX
ADD AX, 3       ; Add 3 to the value in AX
```

In the above example, the program is moving the value 5 into the register AX, then adding 3 to that value.

4. COMMENTS

Comments in assembly language are written to explain parts of the code. They are not executed by the CPU but serve to make the code more understandable to human readers. Comments typically begin with a semicolon (;).

Example:

asm

```
MOV AX, 5       ; Move the value 5 into AX register
```

5. END DIRECTIVE

The END directive marks the end of the program, signaling that there are no more instructions to process.

Example:

```asm

END start
```

2.3 Registers, Memory, and Instructions

At the core of assembly language programming are **registers**, **memory**, and **instructions**. Understanding how these components work is key to writing efficient assembly code.

1. REGISTERS

Registers are small, fast storage locations within the CPU that hold data temporarily while it's being processed. Registers are crucial in assembly programming because they provide quick access to data and are used extensively in calculations, data movement, and control flow. Different types of registers are used for specific purposes, such as holding data or storing memory addresses.

Common types of registers include:

- **Accumulator (AX)**: Used for arithmetic and logic operations.
- **Base Register (BX)**: Often used to hold addresses or data.
- **Index Register (SI, DI)**: Used to store memory addresses during operations like string manipulation.
- **Program Counter (PC)**: Holds the address of the next instruction to be executed.

- **Stack Pointer (SP)**: Points to the current position in the stack, which stores temporary data.

Example:

asm

```
MOV AX, 10     ; Move the value 10 into the AX
register
ADD AX, 5      ; Add 5 to the value in AX
```

In this example, AX is being used as an accumulator to hold and manipulate data.

2. MEMORY

Memory refers to the location where data is stored in a computer system. In assembly language programming, you can interact with memory directly by using memory addresses. These addresses point to specific locations in the system's RAM (Random Access Memory).

Memory can be accessed by:

- **Direct addressing**: Using specific memory addresses.
- **Indirect addressing**: Using a register that holds a memory address.

Example:

asm

```
MOV AX, [5000h]   ; Move the value at memory address
5000h into the AX register
```

In the example above, the program is retrieving the data stored at memory address 5000h and moving it into the register AX.

The instructions in assembly language are commands that tell the CPU what to do. These include operations like:

- **MOV**: Move data from one place to another.
- **ADD**: Add two values together.
- **SUB**: Subtract one value from another.
- **JMP**: Jump to a different instruction (used for loops and branching).
- **CMP**: Compare two values (used in conditional branches).

Example:

asm

```
MOV AX, 10      ; Move the value 10 into AX
ADD AX, 5       ; Add 5 to the value in AX
SUB AX, 2       ; Subtract 2 from AX
```

In this example, the program uses three instructions to modify the value in AX.

2.4 Writing a Basic Assembly Program

Now that we understand the components of assembly language, it's time to write a simple assembly program. For this chapter's hands-on project, we will write a **"Hello World"** program — a classic example used to demonstrate the basics of programming in any language.

Here's how you can write a basic assembly program to display a message on the screen:

```asm
section .data
    msg db 'Hello, World!', 0    ; Define the message

section .text
    global _start                ; Declare the entry point

_start:
    ; Write the message to the screen
    mov eax, 4                   ; 4 is the system call number for sys_write
    mov ebx, 1                   ; 1 is the file descriptor for stdout
    mov ecx, msg                 ; Address of the message
    mov edx, 13                  ; Length of the message
    int 0x80                     ; Call the kernel to write the message

    ; Exit the program
    mov eax, 1                   ; 1 is the system call number for sys_exit
    xor ebx, ebx                 ; Return 0 status
    int 0x80                     ; Call the kernel to exit the program
```

EXPLANATION:

- **section .data**: This section defines the data we want to display, which is the string "Hello, World!".
- **section .text**: This section contains the instructions that make the program run.
- **_start**: This is the entry point of the program, where execution begins.
- **int 0x80**: This is an interrupt that tells the operating system to execute the system calls (like writing to the screen or exiting the program).

2.5 Hands-On Project: Write a Simple "Hello World" Program in Assembly

Now that we've walked through the basic structure of an assembly program, it's time to write our first program together. Follow the steps below to create a "Hello World" program.

1. **Step 1**: Open an assembler (such as NASM or TASM).
2. **Step 2**: Write the assembly code as shown in the previous section.
3. **Step 3**: Assemble and link the code using the assembler tool.
4. **Step 4**: Run the program on your computer and verify that "Hello, World!" is printed to the screen.

Conclusion

In this chapter, we introduced **assembly language,** discussed its structure, and explained how it serves as a bridge between high-level programming languages and machine code. We learned about registers, memory, and instructions, all fundamental concepts for understanding how computers work at the hardware level. Finally, we wrote a simple "Hello World" program in assembly to give you hands-on experience with the concepts we covered.

Assembly language may seem intimidating at first, but with practice, it becomes a powerful tool for anyone looking to master system-level programming and gain a deeper understanding of how computers execute programs. As you continue to work through the examples in this book, you will build the skills necessary to write more complex programs, optimize performance, and work directly with the hardware.

Chapter 3: Machine Language and Binary Code

In this chapter, we are going to explore **machine language**, the lowest level of programming that directly controls the hardware. Machine language is the foundational layer of all software, and understanding it will allow you to grasp how your programs are executed at the hardware level. By the end of this chapter, you'll not only be able to differentiate between machine language and higher-level languages, but also understand how assembly language translates into machine code. You'll also work through real-world examples of how machine code operates and manipulate binary and hexadecimal numbers, which are the languages that the hardware speaks.

3.1 Machine Language vs. Assembly Language

Before we dive deeper into machine language, let's start by distinguishing it from **assembly language**, which we covered in the previous chapter. Both are low-level programming languages, but they differ significantly in terms of their abstraction from the hardware.

WHAT IS MACHINE LANGUAGE?

Machine language, also known as **machine code**, consists of binary instructions that are directly understood by a computer's CPU.

These binary instructions are a series of 0s and 1s, which represent electrical signals or pulses that the hardware can process. Each instruction tells the processor to perform a specific operation, such as adding two numbers, moving data, or making a decision based on a comparison.

Machine code is specific to the architecture of the CPU, meaning that each type of processor has its own set of instructions. For example, an **Intel** processor will have a different set of machine code instructions than an **ARM** processor. The CPU can execute machine code instructions directly without needing any further translation.

WHAT IS ASSEMBLY LANGUAGE?

Assembly language is a symbolic representation of machine code. While machine language uses binary (0s and 1s), assembly language uses human-readable mnemonics (like MOV, ADD, JMP, etc.) to represent the operations that the CPU should perform. Assembly language programs are then converted into machine code by an **assembler**, which is a program that translates the assembly code into the corresponding binary instructions that the CPU can execute.

In summary:

- **Machine Language**: Binary code directly executed by the CPU.
- **Assembly Language**: Human-readable code that is translated into machine code by an assembler.

While assembly language is still quite low-level, it is much more understandable and manageable for humans compared to machine language. However, the real power comes from understanding the underlying machine code, as this is what makes the hardware function.

3.2 Understanding Binary and Hexadecimal Numbers

In both machine language and assembly language, the primary data format is **binary** (base 2), which is made up of two digits: 0 and 1. Computers use binary because they operate using electrical signals that can be either on (1) or off (0).

However, **binary numbers** can be long and cumbersome to work with, especially for humans. To make this easier, we also use **hexadecimal** (base 16), which is a compact way to represent binary numbers. Hexadecimal uses 16 digits: 0-9 for the values 0 to 9, and A-F for the values 10 to 15.

BINARY NUMBERS:

Each digit in a binary number is called a **bit** (short for binary digit). A **byte** consists of 8 bits, and each byte can represent one character in memory, such as a letter or number. For example, the binary number 11010101 represents a specific value in memory. The more bits you have, the larger the range of values you can represent.

HEXADECIMAL NUMBERS:

One hexadecimal digit corresponds to exactly four binary digits (bits), making it more compact and easier to read. For example, the binary number 1101 0101 can be written as the hexadecimal number D5. In this case:

- 1101 in binary is equal to D in hexadecimal (13 in decimal).
- 0101 in binary is equal to 5 in hexadecimal (5 in decimal).

This makes hexadecimal an efficient way to represent binary data. For instance, the 8-bit binary number 11010101 is written as D5 in hexadecimal.

3.3 Translating Assembly to Machine Code

When you write an assembly program, the **assembler** is responsible for translating your symbolic instructions (like MOV AX, 5) into machine code (binary or hexadecimal instructions that the CPU can execute). This translation process is where the abstraction between assembly language and machine language happens.

EXAMPLE TRANSLATION:

Let's look at an example of how an assembly instruction is translated into machine code. The **MOV** instruction in assembly moves data from one location to another. For example:

asm

```
MOV AX, 5
```

This instruction tells the processor to move the value 5 into the register AX. In machine code, this might look something like this (for an x86 processor, for example):

asm

```
B8 05 00 00 00
```

This machine code representation would be read by the CPU and would perform the operation of moving the value 5 into the AX register.

Let's break this down:

- B8 is the opcode for the **MOV** instruction, which tells the CPU to move data into a register.
- 05 00 00 00 is the **immediate value** 5 in little-endian format (a way of representing multi-byte numbers in memory).

INSTRUCTION FORMAT:

Every machine language instruction typically follows a structure, which includes:

1. **Opcode**: Specifies what operation to perform (e.g., MOV, ADD, SUB).
2. **Operands**: Specify the data on which the operation will act (e.g., registers, memory locations, or immediate values).
3. **Addressing Mode**: Defines how the operands are accessed (e.g., direct, indirect, indexed).

The **opcode** tells the CPU what to do (e.g., move data, add values, compare values), and the **operands** provide the specifics of the operation (e.g., the data to be moved or added).

3.4 Real-World Examples: How Machine Code Controls Hardware Operations

Machine code is the fundamental language that allows a CPU to execute instructions and control hardware components. Every action a computer takes, from reading data from a disk to displaying an image on a screen, ultimately relies on machine code instructions.

EXAMPLE 1: READING DATA FROM MEMORY

When a program needs to read data from memory, the machine code instructs the CPU to perform a sequence of steps. For example:

1. The **MOV** instruction is used to load the address of the data into a register.
2. The **LOAD** instruction fetches the data from memory.
3. The **ADD** instruction adds that data to another value.

In machine code, these steps might look like this:

- `MOV AX, [memory_address]` → The `MOV` opcode moves the address of the data into the `AX` register.
- `ADD AX, BX` → The `ADD` opcode adds the data in `BX` to the data in `AX`.

The actual machine code behind these operations is responsible for accessing the memory and performing the necessary computations.

EXAMPLE 2: WRITING DATA TO A PERIPHERAL DEVICE

When writing data to an output device (like a screen), the machine code must follow a specific sequence of operations. This typically involves interacting with the device through memory-mapped I/O or ports. For example:

- A **MOV** instruction is used to load the data to be displayed into a register.
- An **OUT** instruction might be used to send this data to a specific I/O port connected to the screen.

In the case of a display:

asm

```
MOV AX, [data_to_display]   ; Load the data to be
displayed into AX
OUT 0x3F8, AX               ; Send the data to the
display I/O port
```

This series of machine instructions tells the CPU to move the data into the AX register and then send that data to the I/O port that controls the display. The I/O operation directly influences the hardware behavior.

3.5 Hands-On Project: Convert an Assembly Program into Machine Code

Now that we've covered the theory, it's time to put it into practice. In this hands-on project, we'll convert a simple assembly program into machine code using an assembler. We'll write an assembly program, then use the assembler to generate the corresponding machine code.

STEP 1: WRITING THE ASSEMBLY PROGRAM

Let's write a simple program that moves the value 10 into register AX and then stops execution.

asm

```
section .text
    global _start

_start:
    MOV AX, 10  ; Move the value 10 into AX
    MOV BX, AX  ; Move the value in AX into BX
    MOV AX, 1   ; Prepare to exit (sys_exit)
    int 0x80    ; Make the system call to exit
```

STEP 2: ASSEMBLING THE CODE

Using an assembler like **NASM** or **TASM**, you can assemble this program into machine code. To do this, you would run the following command:

bash

```
nasm -f elf64 -o program.o program.asm
```

This command generates an object file (program.o) from the assembly code. We can then link this object file to produce an executable.

STEP 3: GENERATING THE MACHINE CODE

Once you have the object file, use a linker (like **LD** on Linux) to generate the final machine code:

```bash
ld -o program program.o
```

This will produce an executable file, and you can then inspect the raw binary machine code using a **hex editor**.

STEP 4: ANALYZING THE MACHINE CODE

When you open the resulting binary in a hex editor, you'll see a series of bytes corresponding to the machine code that the CPU will execute. For example, the `MOV AX, 10` instruction might appear as:

```hex
B8 0A 00 00 00
```

This is the binary representation of the `MOV AX, 10` instruction. Similarly, other instructions will be translated into their respective binary formats.

Conclusion

In this chapter, we've explored the world of **machine language** and **binary code**, gaining an understanding of how software interacts with hardware at the most fundamental level. We discussed the difference between machine language and assembly language, explained how to translate assembly code into machine code, and explored real-world examples of how machine code controls hardware operations. Finally, through a hands-on project, we converted an assembly program into machine code and analyzed the binary output.

Machine language is the foundation of all computing, and while it may seem distant from the world of high-level programming, understanding it gives you a powerful insight into how your programs run at the hardware level. In the next chapter, we will continue building on these concepts and explore more advanced topics in system architecture.

Chapter 4: Microarchitecture: Building Blocks of a Computer

OBJECTIVE

In this chapter, we will explore **microarchitecture**, which is a critical concept for understanding how a computer's hardware functions and how the processor (CPU) executes instructions. Microarchitecture refers to the design and organization of the components inside the CPU that work together to carry out instructions, perform calculations, and manage the flow of data through the system. We will break down the main components that make up the microarchitecture, understand how they interact with each other, and learn how the overall design of these components impacts the performance of the system. Additionally, we will simulate instruction execution using a simple microarchitecture model as part of a hands-on project.

4.1 What is Microarchitecture?

At its core, **microarchitecture** refers to the layout and organization of the internal components of the **central processing unit (CPU)**. It involves how the various parts of the processor — such as the **Arithmetic Logic Unit (ALU)**, **control unit**, **registers**, and **buses** — are connected and interact with each other. Microarchitecture is often discussed in the context of a specific **processor architecture** (e.g., **x86**, **ARM**, **MIPS**), and the choice of microarchitecture significantly affects the performance, power consumption, and cost of the processor.

To understand microarchitecture, imagine it as the design blueprint for the processor. Just as the layout of a city determines how well traffic flows and services are delivered, the design of a CPU determines how efficiently instructions are executed, how data moves through the system, and how resources are allocated to different tasks. The components of microarchitecture must be carefully optimized to balance **speed**, **throughput**, and **latency**, which are crucial for delivering high-performance computing.

4.2 Understanding the Components of Microarchitecture

There are several key components within the microarchitecture of a CPU, each playing a distinct role in executing instructions and handling data. These components work in concert to ensure that the processor functions efficiently.

1. ARITHMETIC LOGIC UNIT (ALU)

The **Arithmetic Logic Unit (ALU)** is one of the most fundamental components of the CPU. Its primary responsibility is to perform arithmetic and logical operations, such as:

- **Addition, subtraction, multiplication**, and **division** for arithmetic operations.
- **AND**, **OR**, **NOT**, and **XOR** for logical operations.

For example, when an instruction asks the CPU to add two numbers, the ALU performs that operation. The ALU also handles more complex operations like shifting bits and comparing values.

The speed of the ALU is critical for performance because it directly affects how quickly calculations are performed. Modern CPUs may include multiple ALUs to enable parallel processing, further improving performance.

2. CONTROL UNIT (CU)

The **Control Unit (CU)** is the brain of the processor. It manages the flow of data between the ALU, registers, and memory. The CU interprets the instructions in a program and coordinates how the data is processed. It does this by sending control signals to various parts of the CPU, telling them when to read, write, or execute certain operations.

The control unit typically operates using **sequential logic** — it reads each instruction, decodes it to determine what operation to perform, and then triggers the necessary actions. The CU is also responsible for handling jumps and branches in the program (e.g., conditional statements and loops).

3. REGISTERS

Registers are small, fast storage locations inside the CPU that hold data and instructions during processing. Registers can store temporary data, operands for arithmetic operations, memory addresses, and results from instructions. They are essential for fast access to data during program execution.

Common types of registers include:

- **General-purpose registers** (e.g., AX, BX in x86 architecture) are used for storing intermediate results and data.
- **Special-purpose registers** such as the **Program Counter (PC)**, which holds the address of the next instruction to execute, and the **Stack Pointer (SP)**, which keeps track of the stack's top in memory.

Since registers are much faster than accessing data from main memory, they are crucial for maintaining high CPU performance.

A **bus** is a collection of pathways used to transfer data between the various components of the CPU and between the CPU and memory. Buses allow different parts of the system to communicate with each other by sending data signals across these pathways.

Key types of buses include:

- **Data bus**: Carries the actual data between the CPU, memory, and other components.
- **Address bus**: Carries the memory addresses to specify where data is stored or fetched.
- **Control bus**: Sends control signals to manage the operations and timing of the data transfer.

Buses are critical in maintaining high data throughput and ensuring that instructions are executed efficiently.

4.3 The Pipeline and How Instructions Are Processed

One of the most important concepts in modern microarchitecture is the **instruction pipeline**. The pipeline is a technique used to improve the throughput of the CPU by allowing it to process multiple instructions simultaneously, rather than executing one instruction at a time.

In a **pipelined CPU**, the process of executing an instruction is divided into several stages, with each stage performing part of the operation. These stages often include:

1. **Fetch**: Retrieve the next instruction from memory.
2. **Decode**: Interpret the instruction to determine what operation to perform.
3. **Execute**: Perform the operation (e.g., an arithmetic calculation, memory access).
4. **Memory**: Read from or write to memory if necessary.
5. **Write-back**: Write the result back into a register or memory.

At any given time, the CPU can be working on multiple instructions, with each instruction at a different stage of the pipeline. For example, while the CPU is executing an instruction, it can fetch the next instruction and decode it, reducing the time it takes to complete the overall execution of a program.

However, pipelines are not without their challenges. Issues like **data hazards** (where an instruction depends on the result of a previous instruction) and **control hazards** (where the flow of control changes due to a branch) can reduce pipeline efficiency. Modern CPUs use techniques like **out-of-order execution** and **branch prediction** to address these challenges.

4.4 The Role of Cache and Memory Hierarchy

Cache memory plays a crucial role in improving the speed and efficiency of a CPU. Cache is a small, high-speed memory located inside or near the CPU, and it stores frequently used data and instructions to minimize the time spent accessing slower main memory (RAM).

Modern processors employ a **memory hierarchy**, which organizes various levels of cache to optimize access to data:

- **Level 1 Cache (L1)**: This is the smallest and fastest cache, located closest to the CPU cores. It stores frequently accessed instructions and data.
- **Level 2 Cache (L2)**: This cache is larger than L1 and is shared between cores or located per core, offering a balance between speed and size.
- **Level 3 Cache (L3)**: This is a larger, slower cache shared by all cores in multi-core processors, providing a last line of defense before accessing main memory.

The hierarchy ensures that the CPU can access data as quickly as possible, reducing the time it spends waiting for data to be fetched from RAM or slower storage. The better the memory hierarchy, the more effectively the CPU can maintain high performance, particularly in memory-intensive tasks.

4.5 Hands-On Project: Simulate Instruction Execution with a Microarchitecture Model

Now that we've covered the theory of microarchitecture, let's dive into a practical exercise where we simulate the execution of instructions on a basic microarchitecture model. This will help you visualize how the different components of a CPU interact during program execution.

STEP 1: CHOOSE YOUR SIMULATION TOOL

You can use a tool like **Logisim** (for visualizing digital circuits and microarchitecture) or a programming language like Python to create a basic simulation of a CPU pipeline. For this project, we'll use a simple Python-based simulation to model a basic microarchitecture with a small set of instructions.

STEP 2: DEFINE THE COMPONENTS

For this simulation, we'll need to define a basic set of components:

- **Registers**: We'll define a few registers (e.g., AX, BX, CX) to hold data.
- **ALU**: A simple arithmetic logic unit that can perform operations like addition and subtraction.
- **Control Unit**: A basic control unit that decodes instructions and controls data flow.
- **Memory**: A simple memory array to store data.

STEP 3: CREATE A SIMPLE INSTRUCTION SET

For this simulation, we'll use a minimal instruction set:

- `MOV R, val`: Move a value into a register.
- `ADD R1, R2`: Add the values in two registers and store the result in the first register.
- `JMP addr`: Jump to a different instruction address (used for simulating loops).

STEP 4: WRITE THE SIMULATION CODE

Here's an example of a simple simulation in Python:

```python
class CPU:
    def __init__(self):
        self.registers = {"AX": 0, "BX": 0, "CX": 0}
        self.memory = [0] * 256  # Simple memory
model
        self.pc = 0  # Program Counter

    def fetch(self):
        # Fetch the next instruction
        instruction = instructions[self.pc]
        self.pc += 1
        return instruction

    def decode(self, instruction):
        # Decode the instruction
        parts = instruction.split()
        return parts

    def execute(self, decoded_instruction):
        # Execute the instruction
        if decoded_instruction[0] == "MOV":
            self.registers[decoded_instruction[1]] =
int(decoded_instruction[2])
        elif decoded_instruction[0] == "ADD":
            self.registers[decoded_instruction[1]] +=
self.registers[decoded_instruction[2]]

# Sample instructions (MOV, ADD)
instructions = ["MOV AX, 10", "MOV BX, 20", "ADD AX,
BX"]

# Initialize CPU
cpu = CPU()

# Simulate instruction execution
while cpu.pc < len(instructions):
    instruction = cpu.fetch()
    decoded = cpu.decode(instruction)
    cpu.execute(decoded)

print(cpu.registers)
```

This simple code snippet simulates the fetch-decode-execute cycle of a CPU. It shows how instructions are fetched from memory, decoded, and executed, affecting the CPU's registers.

Run the simulation and observe how the registers change after each instruction. For example:

- After the first instruction `MOV AX, 10`, the `AX` register will hold the value `10`.
- After the second instruction `MOV BX, 20`, the `BX` register will hold the value `20`.
- After the third instruction `ADD AX, BX`, the value of `AX` will become `30` (10 + 20).

This project helps you visualize the basic workings of a CPU as it processes instructions in a simplified microarchitecture.

Conclusion

In this chapter, we have introduced **microarchitecture** and explored its role in the performance of a system. We discussed the components that make up the CPU, such as the **ALU**, **control unit**, **registers**, and **buses**, and how they interact during the execution of instructions. We also delved into the concept of the **instruction pipeline** and how modern CPUs use multiple stages to execute instructions efficiently. Finally, we explored the role of **cache** and **memory hierarchy** in speeding up data access and improving performance.

By completing the hands-on project, you gained a deeper understanding of how instructions are processed at the microarchitecture level. This knowledge is essential for anyone interested in system-level programming, optimization, or hardware design.

Chapter 5: The CPU: The Brain of the System

In this chapter, we will delve into the **Central Processing Unit (CPU)**, often referred to as the "brain" of a computer. The CPU is the most important component in any system, responsible for executing instructions, performing calculations, and managing data flow. It drives the processing of tasks and serves as the cornerstone of system performance. In this chapter, we'll explore the design and function of the CPU, the instruction sets it uses, the different CPU modes (protected, real, and virtual), and how clock cycles affect performance. Additionally, we'll include a hands-on project that simulates a CPU's role in executing simple operations to help reinforce these concepts.

5.1 Understanding CPU Design and Function

The **CPU** is essentially the heart of a computing system. It is the hardware responsible for interpreting and executing instructions from the system's software. The CPU coordinates the activities of the computer, interacts with memory and input/output devices, and processes the data necessary for the system to function.

CPU Design: The Basic Architecture

The design of a CPU is composed of several key components, each of which has a specific role in the processing of instructions. These components include:

- **Control Unit (CU)**: The CU manages and coordinates the execution of instructions. It fetches instructions from memory, decodes them, and then directs the rest of the CPU on what operations to perform. The CU also handles branching and looping within programs.
- **Arithmetic Logic Unit (ALU)**: The ALU is responsible for performing all arithmetic and logical operations in the CPU. This includes addition, subtraction, multiplication, division, and comparisons (greater than, less than, equal to).
- **Registers**: Registers are small, high-speed storage locations within the CPU that temporarily hold data. They are used to store intermediate values, memory addresses, or data that the CPU is currently processing.
- **Buses**: A bus is a communication pathway that transfers data between the CPU, memory, and other components. There are various types of buses, such as the data bus (which carries data) and the address bus (which carries memory addresses).

The CPU's Role in Data Processing

When the CPU executes a program, it goes through a cycle of fetching instructions, decoding them, and then executing them. This cycle is known as the **fetch-decode-execute cycle** and is fundamental to the operation of the CPU.

1. **Fetch**: The CPU fetches the next instruction from memory using the program counter (PC), which keeps track of the memory address of the next instruction.

2. **Decode**: The instruction is decoded by the control unit to determine what operation it represents and which components of the CPU need to be involved.
3. **Execute**: The CPU performs the operation, whether it's an arithmetic calculation, a data movement operation, or a memory access operation.

This cycle continues until the program is finished or the CPU is instructed to halt.

5.2 Instruction Sets and CPU Modes

INSTRUCTION SETS

The **instruction set** is the collection of all the operations that a CPU can perform. Each CPU architecture (e.g., **x86**, **ARM**) has its own unique instruction set, and these instructions are what programmers use to interact with the hardware. Some common instruction set operations include:

- **MOV**: Move data from one location to another.
- **ADD**: Perform addition.
- **SUB**: Perform subtraction.
- **JMP**: Jump to another instruction location (used for loops and branches).

The **instruction set architecture (ISA)** is the set of machine-level instructions that the CPU can execute. For example, the **x86 architecture** is widely used in PCs and has a specific set of instructions that are different from the **ARM architecture**, which is commonly used in mobile devices.

CPU MODES: REAL, PROTECTED, AND VIRTUAL

Modern CPUs have different operating **modes**, which define how the CPU interacts with the system's memory and how it handles tasks. These modes include:

1. **Real Mode**:
   - **Real Mode** is the simplest CPU mode and is used by older processors. In real mode, the CPU can only address up to 1 MB of memory (because it uses a 20-bit address bus), and it cannot implement memory protection or multitasking.
   - **Real Mode** is used during the initial stages of booting a computer, as it allows for direct access to hardware.
2. **Protected Mode**:
   - **Protected Mode** was introduced with the **Intel 80286** processor and allows the CPU to access more memory (more than 1 MB), manage multiple programs (multitasking), and prevent one program from interfering with others.
   - In protected mode, the CPU can **protect** memory regions, ensuring that programs don't accidentally modify or access memory allocated to other programs. This is crucial for running modern operating systems like Windows, Linux, or macOS, which require the ability to run multiple applications at once without conflicts.
3. **Virtual Mode**:
   - **Virtual Mode** extends protected mode to allow multiple virtual machines (VMs) to run on a single physical machine. Each virtual machine behaves as though it has its own independent CPU and memory, but in reality, they share the same physical resources.
   - Virtualization is a key feature of modern operating systems and is used in cloud computing, server

management, and virtualization platforms like VMware, VirtualBox, and Hyper-V.

Each of these modes provides different levels of access to system resources, and the CPU automatically switches between modes depending on the task at hand. For example, the operating system kernel typically runs in protected mode, while user applications might run in virtual mode.

5.3 Clock Cycles and Performance Metrics

The **clock cycle** is the fundamental unit of time in a CPU. It is the rate at which the CPU executes instructions, and it is determined by the **system clock**. The system clock generates regular pulses that synchronize the operation of all components in the system. Each clock cycle is a single pulse, and the CPU typically processes one instruction (or part of an instruction) per clock cycle.

HOW CLOCK SPEED AFFECTS PERFORMANCE

The **clock speed** (measured in **Hertz**, or cycles per second) determines how many cycles the CPU can execute in a given amount of time. Modern CPUs have clock speeds measured in gigahertz (GHz), which means billions of clock cycles per second. Higher clock speeds generally result in faster performance, but there are other factors to consider, such as the number of CPU cores, the instruction set, and the architecture.

For example, a CPU running at **3 GHz** can theoretically execute 3 billion clock cycles per second. However, not every instruction takes exactly one cycle — some instructions require multiple cycles. Thus, the number of cycles per instruction (CPI) is an important metric when evaluating performance.

PERFORMANCE METRICS

There are several key performance metrics that help us understand how efficiently a CPU is working:

- **Cycles Per Instruction (CPI)**: This is the average number of clock cycles required to execute an instruction. The lower the CPI, the better the CPU performs, as it can complete instructions faster.
- **Instructions Per Cycle (IPC)**: This measures how many instructions the CPU can execute per clock cycle. A higher IPC typically correlates with better performance.
- **Clock Speed (GHz)**: A higher clock speed generally means that the CPU can perform more operations per second.
- **Throughput**: This measures how much data the CPU can process in a given period. It's influenced by the CPU's clock speed, IPC, and the number of cores in the processor.
- **Latency**: This measures the time it takes for the CPU to complete a single instruction or operation. Lower latency results in quicker task completion.

By considering these factors together, we can get a sense of how well a CPU performs in a given task, whether it's gaming, data processing, or running multiple applications simultaneously.

5.4 Hands-On Project: Simulate a CPU's Role in Executing Simple Operations

Now that we've learned about the fundamental components of the CPU, let's get hands-on and simulate how a CPU executes simple operations.

In this project, we'll write a simple Python program to simulate the execution of basic arithmetic operations by the CPU. We'll include components like the **Arithmetic Logic Unit (ALU)**, **registers**, and **memory**, and demonstrate how they work together in the **fetch-decode-execute cycle**.

STEP 1: DEFINE THE CPU COMPONENTS

We'll start by creating a basic CPU class that includes registers, an ALU, and a program counter. The program counter will keep track of the instruction pointer as the CPU executes instructions.

```python
class CPU:
    def __init__(self):
        self.registers = {"AX": 0, "BX": 0, "CX": 0}
# Simple registers
        self.memory = [0] * 256  # Simple memory
model
        self.pc = 0  # Program Counter
        self.cycle = 0  # Clock cycle counter

    def fetch(self):
        # Fetch the next instruction from memory
        instruction = instructions[self.pc]
        self.pc += 1
        return instruction

    def decode(self, instruction):
        # Decode the instruction
```

```python
        parts = instruction.split()
        return parts

    def execute(self, decoded_instruction):
        # Execute the decoded instruction
        if decoded_instruction[0] == "MOV":
            self.registers[decoded_instruction[1]] =
int(decoded_instruction[2])
        elif decoded_instruction[0] == "ADD":
            self.registers[decoded_instruction[1]] +=
self.registers[decoded_instruction[2]]
        elif decoded_instruction[0] == "SUB":
            self.registers[decoded_instruction[1]] -=
self.registers[decoded_instruction[2]]

    def run(self):
        # Run the CPU until all instructions are
executed
        while self.pc < len(instructions):
            instruction = self.fetch()
            decoded = self.decode(instruction)
            self.execute(decoded)
            self.cycle += 1
            print(f"Cycle {self.cycle}:
{self.registers}")

# Sample instructions (MOV, ADD, SUB)
instructions = ["MOV AX, 10", "MOV BX, 20", "ADD AX,
BX", "SUB BX, AX"]

# Initialize the CPU
cpu = CPU()

# Run the simulation
cpu.run()
```

STEP 2: SIMULATE THE EXECUTION

In this simulation, the program follows these steps:

1. The CPU fetches the next instruction from memory (the
    instruction set we've defined).

2. The instruction is decoded to determine what operation it represents (e.g., MOV, ADD, or SUB).
3. The operation is executed using the CPU's ALU and registers, with the results being stored in the registers.

After running the simulation, you should see output that shows how the CPU's registers change after each instruction. For example:

yaml

```
Cycle 1: {'AX': 10, 'BX': 0, 'CX': 0}
Cycle 2: {'AX': 10, 'BX': 20, 'CX': 0}
Cycle 3: {'AX': 30, 'BX': 20, 'CX': 0}
Cycle 4: {'AX': 30, 'BX': 10, 'CX': 0}
```

This simple simulation gives us insight into how a CPU processes instructions and how the data in the registers changes throughout the execution.

Conclusion

In this chapter, we've explored the **Central Processing Unit (CPU)** in-depth, covering its components, design, and role in executing instructions. We discussed the importance of the **control unit**, **arithmetic logic unit (ALU)**, **registers**, and **buses**, all of which work together to enable the CPU to perform its tasks. We also learned about the different **CPU modes** (real, protected, virtual) and how they affect memory access and multitasking.

Finally, through a hands-on project, we simulated a simple CPU's role in executing basic operations like MOV, ADD, and SUB. This practical project allowed us to visualize how the CPU fetches, decodes, and executes instructions.

Chapter 6: Memory Systems and Hierarchy

In this chapter, we will dive into the **memory systems** of a computer and how they interact with each other to provide efficient data storage and retrieval. We will explore the different **types of memory** (such as **registers**, **cache**, **RAM**, and **virtual memory**), how memory is **addressed**, and the role of **paging** in memory management. Additionally, we will discuss how memory is organized in a hierarchical system and how these hierarchies influence **system performance**. Finally, we'll undertake a hands-on project where we implement a basic **memory manager** in **assembly language** to see how memory management works at a low level.

6.1 Types of Memory: Registers, Cache, RAM, and Virtual Memory

Memory is one of the most critical components of a computer system. It allows the system to store data temporarily while it is being processed, and it ensures that the CPU has quick access to the data it needs. There are different types of memory, each with its unique characteristics and purposes. Understanding these different types and how they interact is key to understanding how a system performs.

1. REGISTERS

Registers are the fastest and smallest form of memory in a computer system. They are located directly inside the CPU, providing quick access to data that is actively being processed. Registers hold data that the CPU is currently working on, such as values for arithmetic operations, addresses, and intermediate results.

There are generally two types of registers:

- **General-purpose registers**: These hold data that is used in calculations or operations.
- **Special-purpose registers**: These include the **Program Counter (PC)**, which keeps track of the next instruction to execute, and the **Stack Pointer (SP)**, which points to the current position in the call stack.

Because registers are so close to the CPU, they are extremely fast but limited in size. There are typically only a few registers in a CPU, so they can only store a small amount of data at any given time.

2. CACHE MEMORY

Cache memory sits between the CPU and the main memory (RAM), providing a fast temporary storage for frequently accessed data. Cache is much faster than RAM and is used to store data that is repeatedly accessed, reducing the need for the CPU to access the slower main memory.

Modern CPUs typically have several levels of cache:

- **L1 Cache**: This is the smallest and fastest cache, located closest to the CPU cores. It stores small amounts of data that are frequently accessed.

- **L2 Cache**: This is slightly larger and slower than L1 but still much faster than RAM. It is often shared between cores or located per core, depending on the processor design.
- **L3 Cache**: This is the largest and slowest of the three levels of cache, but still much faster than RAM. It is typically shared by all CPU cores.

The cache is vital for optimizing performance, especially for tasks that involve repetitive data access, such as running applications or playing games.

3. RAM (RANDOM ACCESS MEMORY)

RAM is the main memory of a computer, where data is stored while the CPU is processing it. It is volatile, meaning it loses all data when the computer is turned off. RAM provides much more storage capacity than registers or cache but is slower to access.

RAM is essential for storing programs and data that need to be accessed quickly by the CPU. The amount of RAM in a system directly affects its performance — more RAM allows the system to run more programs simultaneously and handle more data at once.

There are different types of RAM, including:

- **DRAM (Dynamic RAM)**: This is the most common type of RAM. It needs to be refreshed regularly to maintain the data stored in it.
- **SRAM (Static RAM)**: This type of RAM is faster and more reliable than DRAM but is more expensive and uses more power.

Virtual memory allows the system to use hard drive space as additional memory, effectively "expanding" the amount of RAM available. When the physical RAM is full, the operating system moves less-used data to the hard drive in a space called the **swap file** or **page file**.

Virtual memory is important for running large applications or multiple applications simultaneously without running out of memory. However, since accessing data from the hard drive is much slower than accessing data from RAM, relying heavily on virtual memory can result in significant performance degradation.

The operating system uses a process called **paging** to manage virtual memory, breaking data into small blocks called **pages** and swapping these pages in and out of physical memory as needed.

6.2 Memory Addressing and Paging

Memory addressing refers to how data is accessed in memory. The CPU needs to know where data is located in memory so it can retrieve or store it. In modern systems, memory is organized into address spaces, with each address representing a unique location in memory.

1. DIRECT ADDRESSING AND INDIRECT ADDRESSING

In **direct addressing**, the memory address is explicitly specified in the instruction, and the CPU can access the data directly. For example:

```asm
MOV AX, [1000h]    ; Move data from memory address
1000h into AX register
```

Here, the CPU accesses the memory address `1000h` directly.

In **indirect addressing**, a register or memory location holds the address of the data to be accessed. For example:

```asm
MOV BX, [SI]       ; Move data from the memory address
in SI register into BX
```

In this case, the data is not stored at `SI` itself but rather at the address pointed to by `SI`.

2. PAGING

Paging is a memory management scheme that allows the operating system to break the physical memory into small fixed-size blocks called **pages**. The virtual memory is divided into **virtual pages**, which are mapped to physical pages in RAM by the **page table**.

Each time the CPU needs to access data, the operating system checks the page table to see if the page is in physical memory. If it is, the data is retrieved quickly; if not, the system uses **page swapping** to move pages between physical memory and the swap file on the hard disk.

Paging helps manage large amounts of memory efficiently, especially in systems with limited physical RAM, but it can lead to performance issues when the system relies too much on swapping.

6.3 Memory Management: How Data is Retrieved and Stored

Memory management involves controlling and coordinating the memory resources in a system. The operating system uses different algorithms to manage memory allocation, deallocation, and the efficient retrieval and storage of data.

1. MEMORY ALLOCATION

Memory allocation is the process of assigning a portion of memory to a program or task. This can be done in several ways:

- **Contiguous Allocation**: Memory is allocated in a single contiguous block, making access fast but requiring large contiguous memory spaces.
- **Non-contiguous Allocation**: Memory is divided into smaller chunks that can be scattered throughout physical memory. This method is more flexible but can lead to fragmentation.
- **Dynamic Allocation**: Programs can request memory dynamically at runtime, with the operating system allocating memory as needed.

2. MEMORY DEALLOCATION

Once a program no longer needs a chunk of memory, the memory is deallocated. The operating system marks the memory as free and available for reuse. Efficient deallocation is essential for preventing memory leaks, where memory is never returned to the system and eventually leads to a shortage of available memory.

3. Memory Protection

Modern operating systems use **memory protection** to prevent one program from accessing or modifying the memory of another program. This is achieved through the use of **address spaces**, which separate each program's memory from others, ensuring that programs run independently without interfering with each other.

4. Garbage Collection

In some systems, particularly with high-level programming languages, **garbage collection** is used to automatically deallocate memory that is no longer needed. The garbage collector periodically scans memory for objects that are no longer referenced and frees that memory.

6.4 Real-World Applications: Optimizing Memory for Embedded Systems

In embedded systems, memory is often limited and performance is critical. Optimizing memory use is essential to ensure that the system runs efficiently within the constraints of its hardware.

1. Memory Optimization in Embedded Systems

To optimize memory in embedded systems:

- **Use Fixed-size Memory Pools**: Instead of dynamically allocating and deallocating memory, which can be slow and prone to fragmentation, fixed-size memory pools allocate a predefined chunk of memory.

- **Minimize Memory Footprint**: Embedded systems typically have small amounts of RAM, so developers must minimize the memory footprint of applications by reducing the size of data structures and avoiding large, memory-hogging libraries.
- **Memory-Mapped I/O**: Many embedded systems use memory-mapped I/O to control hardware devices, allowing the CPU to read and write to hardware registers as if they were part of memory. This technique simplifies programming and improves performance.

2. MEMORY MANAGEMENT IN REAL-TIME SYSTEMS

In real-time embedded systems, **real-time memory management** is crucial to meet the system's timing requirements. The system must allocate and deallocate memory with predictable timing, ensuring that the CPU can meet strict deadlines for processing tasks.

6.5 Hands-On Project: Implement a Memory Manager in Assembly Language

In this hands-on project, we will implement a basic **memory manager** in **assembly language**. The goal of this project is to demonstrate how memory can be allocated and deallocated manually, using low-level assembly code to simulate a memory manager.

STEP 1: DEFINE THE MEMORY MODEL

We'll simulate a simple memory model using an array of bytes to represent memory. Each byte can either be marked as **free** or **allocated**.

```asm
section .data
    memory db 100 dup(0)   ; Simulate 100 bytes of
memory, all free (0 = free, 1 = allocated)
```

STEP 2: IMPLEMENT MEMORY ALLOCATION

To allocate memory, we need to find a free block of memory and mark it as allocated. For simplicity, we'll implement a **first-fit** allocation strategy, where the first available block of memory is used.

```asm
allocate:
    ; Find the first free block in memory
    mov esi, 0
find_free:
    cmp byte [memory + esi], 0  ; Check if the memory
at this position is free
    je allocate_found
    inc esi
    cmp esi, 100  ; Check if we've scanned all the
memory
    jl find_free
    ret

allocate_found:
    mov byte [memory + esi], 1  ; Mark the memory as
allocated
    ret
```

STEP 3: IMPLEMENT MEMORY DEALLOCATION

To deallocate memory, we simply mark the memory block as free.

```asm
deallocate:
```

```asm
    ; Find the allocated block in memory
    mov esi, 0
find_allocated:
    cmp byte [memory + esi], 1  ; Check if the memory
at this position is allocated
    je deallocate_found
    inc esi
    cmp esi, 100
    jl find_allocated
    ret

deallocate_found:
    mov byte [memory + esi], 0  ; Mark the memory as
free
    ret
```

STEP 4: RUN THE MEMORY MANAGER

Now that we've implemented the basic memory management functions, we can write a program that allocates and deallocates memory to simulate a basic memory manager in action.

asm

```
section .text
    global _start

_start:
    ; Allocate memory
    call allocate
    ; Deallocate memory
    call deallocate
```

STEP 5: TESTING THE MEMORY MANAGER

Once the memory manager is implemented, test it by simulating memory allocation and deallocation. You'll be able to observe how memory is managed at the low level and gain an appreciation for how real memory management works under the hood.

Conclusion

In this chapter, we explored **memory systems** and **memory hierarchy,** focusing on the different types of memory (such as registers, cache, RAM, and virtual memory) and how they affect system performance. We discussed memory addressing, paging, and the crucial role of memory management in ensuring efficient data retrieval and storage.

Through a hands-on project, we implemented a basic **memory manager** in assembly language, simulating how memory is allocated and deallocated. This project gave us a low-level understanding of memory management, which is essential for optimizing performance, particularly in systems with limited resources, such as embedded systems.

Chapter 7: Input/Output Systems and Hardware Control

OBJECTIVE

In this chapter, we will explore the **Input/Output (I/O) systems** and **hardware control** that enable a computer's processor to interact with peripheral devices like keyboards, screens, printers, and disk drives. I/O systems are critical for a computer's functionality, as they serve as the interface between the computer's internal components and the external world. We will discuss how I/O operations work, the role of **Direct Memory Access (DMA)** and **interrupts**, and how communication happens between hardware components. By the end of this chapter, we will also undertake a hands-on project in **assembly language** to interact with simple I/O devices, such as a keyboard or a screen.

7.1 How I/O Operations Work

At its core, **I/O operations** allow the CPU to communicate with external devices. These devices include input devices like keyboards and mice, output devices like screens and printers, and storage devices like hard drives and SSDs. Without a proper I/O system, the computer would be limited to processing data internally without any external interaction.

THE BASICS OF I/O OPERATIONS

I/O operations involve the **transfer of data** between the computer's processor and peripheral devices. These operations can be broadly classified into two types:

1. **Input Operations**: These are operations where data is received from external devices and transferred into the computer's memory. For example, pressing a key on a keyboard is an input operation that sends data to the CPU for processing.
2. **Output Operations**: These operations involve sending data from the computer's memory to external devices. For instance, displaying text on a screen or sending data to a printer is an output operation.

I/O operations typically occur through **ports**, which are hardware interfaces that allow data to flow between the CPU and peripheral devices. Communication through these ports can happen through two primary methods: **polling** and **interrupts**.

POLLING VS. INTERRUPTS

- **Polling**: In polling, the CPU repeatedly checks the status of an I/O device at regular intervals to see if it is ready to send or receive data. For example, the CPU might check the keyboard to see if a key has been pressed. While polling is simple, it can be inefficient because it requires the CPU to constantly check devices, even when they have no data to send.
- **Interrupts**: Interrupts offer a more efficient approach. Instead of the CPU constantly checking devices, the I/O device sends an interrupt signal to the CPU when it needs attention (for example, when a key is pressed on the keyboard). The CPU pauses its current operations and handles the interrupt, responding to the I/O device's request.

Afterward, the CPU resumes its previous task. Interrupts improve efficiency and allow for more responsive systems.

I/O devices communicate with the CPU via **I/O ports**. These ports are managed by specialized controllers, which handle the details of communication. The data is transferred through a **bus**, which is a set of pathways that carry data between the CPU, memory, and I/O devices. There are several types of buses, including:

- **Data Bus**: Carries the actual data between components.
- **Address Bus**: Carries the addresses of where the data needs to go in memory or I/O space.
- **Control Bus**: Carries control signals that manage the timing and coordination of data transfers.

7.2 Direct Memory Access (DMA) and Interrupts

DIRECT MEMORY ACCESS (DMA)

DMA is a method that allows certain hardware subsystems (like a disk drive or a sound card) to communicate directly with the main memory, bypassing the CPU. This is particularly useful for high-speed data transfers, such as moving large chunks of data between the memory and storage devices without taxing the CPU.

With DMA, the device requesting the data transfer sends a request to the DMA controller, which then directly manages the transfer of data between memory and the peripheral. This allows the CPU to perform other tasks while the data is being moved, significantly improving system efficiency, especially for tasks like reading from a disk or streaming video data.

How DMA Works:

1. The CPU sends a DMA request to the DMA controller, specifying the memory location and the peripheral device involved.
2. The DMA controller takes over the data transfer process.
3. The data is transferred from the I/O device to the memory (or vice versa) directly, without involving the CPU.
4. Once the transfer is complete, the DMA controller sends an interrupt to notify the CPU that the operation is finished.

INTERRUPTS AND INTERRUPT HANDLING

Interrupts play a crucial role in managing I/O operations efficiently. When a device needs attention, it sends an interrupt signal to the CPU, temporarily halting its current operations. The CPU responds by entering an **interrupt service routine (ISR)**, which is a piece of code that handles the interrupt and processes the device's request. Once the ISR is completed, the CPU resumes its normal operations.

Interrupts can be categorized into:

- **Hardware Interrupts**: These come from external devices, such as a keyboard, mouse, or timer, indicating that they need attention.
- **Software Interrupts**: These are initiated by programs to request certain services from the operating system, like system calls.

Interrupt handling improves system responsiveness and allows the CPU to focus on other tasks instead of continuously checking for device readiness.

7.3 Communication Between Hardware Components

The communication between the CPU and hardware components, including I/O devices, happens through a well-defined set of protocols and control mechanisms. The CPU interacts with various controllers (such as the **keyboard controller** or **graphics controller**) to manage the data flow.

MEMORY-MAPPED I/O VS. PORT-MAPPED I/O

- **Memory-Mapped I/O**: In memory-mapped I/O, peripherals are treated like memory locations. Each device has a specific address range in the memory address space, and the CPU can interact with them using standard memory instructions like MOV. This method simplifies communication but requires careful management to avoid conflicts.
- **Port-Mapped I/O**: In port-mapped I/O, I/O devices are assigned to specific I/O ports, separate from memory. The CPU uses special I/O instructions (like IN and OUT) to interact with the devices. Port-mapped I/O provides a distinct address space for I/O operations, reducing the complexity of memory management.

BUS ARBITRATION AND DATA TRANSFER PROTOCOLS

When multiple components (such as the CPU, memory, and I/O devices) share the same bus, it is important to manage how data is transferred to avoid conflicts. **Bus arbitration** is the process of determining which device gets access to the bus at any given time. Devices send requests to the arbiter, which grants access based on priorities.

Data transfer protocols, such as **Serial Communication** (where data is transferred one bit at a time over a single channel) and **Parallel Communication** (where multiple bits are transferred simultaneously), are used to ensure data is communicated effectively between devices.

7.4 Hands-On Project: Write Assembly Code to Interact with a Simple I/O Device (Keyboard, Screen)

Now that we've covered the theory of I/O systems and hardware control, it's time for a practical project. In this project, we will write simple **assembly code** to interact with two I/O devices: a **keyboard** and a **screen**.

STEP 1: SETTING UP THE ENVIRONMENT

For this project, we will use an **x86** processor in **real mode** and work in an environment like **DOSBox** or a simple **bare-metal system** where we can directly interact with hardware without operating system interference. We'll write assembly code using the **NASM** assembler and run it in a simple real-mode environment.

STEP 2: READING INPUT FROM THE KEYBOARD

To read input from the keyboard, we will use the **keyboard controller**, which is mapped to specific I/O ports. In real-mode assembly, we can use **IN** and **OUT** instructions to send and receive data to and from the keyboard controller.

Here's a simple program to read a key press from the keyboard:

```asm
asm

section .data
    msg db 'Press a key: $'  ; Display this message

section .text
    global _start

_start:
    ; Output the message
    mov ah, 0x09     ; BIOS interrupt to display
string
    lea dx, [msg]
    int 0x21

    ; Wait for a key press
    mov ah, 0x00     ; BIOS interrupt to wait for a
key press
    int 0x16         ; Keyboard interrupt

    ; Store the key press in AL register
    ; AL register now contains the ASCII code of the
key
    mov dl, al       ;  the key press to DL for
display
    mov ah, 0x02     ; BIOS interrupt to display
character
    int 0x21

    ; Exit
    mov ah, 0x4C     ; DOS interrupt to terminate
program
    int 0x21
```

STEP 3: OUTPUTTING DATA TO THE SCREEN

The **screen** is another I/O device that the CPU can control. To output data to the screen in real mode, we typically use BIOS interrupts.

In the example above, the `int 0x21` interrupt with function `0x02` is used to display a single character. This interrupt takes the character in the **DL register** and displays it on the screen.

STEP 4: FULL PROGRAM EXECUTION

The complete program reads a key from the keyboard and immediately displays the corresponding character on the screen. When you run this program in a real-mode environment, it will:

1. Display the prompt "Press a key:"
2. Wait for a key press.
3. Display the pressed key on the screen.

This interaction demonstrates the fundamental I/O operations using assembly language and gives you a basic understanding of how hardware control works at the lowest level.

7.5 Conclusion

In this chapter, we have explored the **Input/Output (I/O) systems** and **hardware control** that form the bridge between a computer's processor and peripheral devices. We discussed how I/O operations work, the role of **Direct Memory Access (DMA)**, and how interrupts help in efficiently managing I/O operations. We also examined the communication methods between hardware components and the different types of I/O systems, including memory-mapped and port-mapped I/O.

Through the hands-on project, we gained practical experience by writing **assembly code** to interact with simple I/O devices such as the **keyboard** and **screen**. This exercise provided us with insight into how low-level I/O operations are handled by the processor and the critical role that hardware control plays in the functioning of a computer.

Chapter 8: Performance Tuning: Optimizing System Speed

OBJECTIVE

In this chapter, we'll dive into the world of **performance tuning** and explore techniques used to enhance the efficiency of computer systems. System performance directly impacts the user experience, whether you're dealing with a simple application, a server farm, or high-performance computing (HPC) environments. The goal of performance tuning is to ensure that the system runs as efficiently as possible, with minimal bottlenecks and optimal use of resources. We'll cover how to identify bottlenecks, utilize **profiling tools** for performance analysis, employ **code optimization techniques**, and explore **real-world applications** in industries like server farms and HPC. Finally, we will work on a **hands-on project** to optimize an **assembly program** for speed, helping you put these concepts into practice.

8.1 Bottlenecks and How to Identify Them

A **bottleneck** occurs when a part of the system significantly limits the overall performance, slowing down the entire process. Bottlenecks can happen at various points in a system: the CPU, memory, storage, network, or even the software. To optimize system performance, it's crucial to first identify where the bottlenecks are occurring.

1. **CPU Bottleneck**:
   - This happens when the CPU is unable to process instructions fast enough. It can occur due to slow CPU clock speed, inefficient code, or lack of parallelism.
   - Common indicators of a CPU bottleneck include high CPU utilization (close to 100%) and long processing times for tasks that require substantial computation.
2. **Memory Bottleneck**:
   - Memory bottlenecks occur when the CPU is waiting for data to be fetched from memory, resulting in slower execution. This can be caused by insufficient RAM, slow access speeds (e.g., using hard disk drives instead of solid-state drives), or memory fragmentation.
   - Signs of memory bottlenecks include high memory usage, long load times for programs, or swapping data between RAM and disk storage.
3. **Storage Bottleneck**:
   - A storage bottleneck occurs when data retrieval or writing speeds from storage devices (HDDs, SSDs) are too slow for the processing needs of the system. This is particularly evident in I/O-heavy tasks like large file transfers, video rendering, or database queries.
   - Indicators include slow file access speeds, long read/write times, and noticeable delays when accessing files or databases.
4. **Network Bottleneck**:
   - In systems that rely heavily on network communication (such as cloud-based applications or distributed systems), a network bottleneck can significantly degrade performance. This could be due to limited bandwidth, high latency, or network congestion.

- You can detect network bottlenecks by monitoring network traffic, high latency, or slow response times during data transfers.

5. **Software Bottleneck**:
   - Software bottlenecks arise from inefficient algorithms, poor coding practices, or suboptimal use of system resources. These bottlenecks often show up in code with excessive loops, unnecessary computations, or improper resource management.
   - Indicators include slow execution of specific functions or tasks, especially those that handle large volumes of data or perform complex calculations.

HOW TO IDENTIFY BOTTLENECKS

1. **Monitor System Performance**:
   - Use performance monitoring tools like **Task Manager (Windows)** or **Activity Monitor (macOS)** to observe CPU, memory, disk, and network usage. These tools can help identify which part of the system is being overutilized.

2. **Profiling**:
   - Profiling tools allow you to analyze the execution time of various parts of your program, pinpointing the sections that are consuming the most resources.
   - Some popular profiling tools include:
     - **Linux `top` and `htop`**: Used to monitor overall system resource usage, including CPU, memory, and processes.
     - **Intel VTune**: A performance profiler for analyzing CPU performance and identifying hotspots in applications.
     - **gProfiler**: A sampling profiler for visualizing performance issues in software.

3. **Benchmarking**:

- o Benchmarking tools like **Geekbench**, **PassMark**, and **Cinebench** provide insights into how well a system performs under stress. They help identify specific hardware or software limitations by running controlled tests that simulate different workloads.
4. **Examine Logs**:
    - o Logs from applications or system services can reveal performance issues. By examining logs, you can find errors, delays, or resource-hogging activities that might contribute to bottlenecks.

8.2 Using Profiling Tools for Performance Analysis

Profiling is a critical step in performance tuning. It involves measuring the time and resources consumed by specific sections of code or hardware components. Profiling tools allow developers to gather detailed performance data, helping them pinpoint exactly where the system is slowing down.

KEY PROFILING TOOLS AND THEIR USES

1. **CPU Profilers**:
    - o **gProfiler**: A tool that helps identify the performance bottlenecks in your software by showing you where your code spends the most time. It provides detailed reports of CPU usage, including function call counts, execution times, and memory usage.
    - o **Intel VTune Profiler**: A powerful profiling tool that helps identify CPU and memory performance bottlenecks. It allows developers to visualize CPU utilization, cache misses, and branch mispredictions.

2. **Memory Profilers**:
   o **Valgrind**: A tool used to analyze memory usage and identify issues like memory leaks, memory corruption, and inefficient memory access patterns. It provides detailed insights into how memory is allocated, used, and freed within your application.
   o **Memory Profiler for Python**: A Python-specific profiler that allows developers to track memory allocation and usage within a Python program.
3. **I/O Profilers**:
   o **iostat**: A Linux-based tool that helps monitor I/O performance, including disk reads and writes. By using `iostat`, developers can determine if slow disk access is contributing to system bottlenecks.
   o **dstat**: A versatile tool that provides real-time monitoring of system resources, including I/O performance, CPU usage, and disk throughput.
4. **Network Profilers**:
   o **Wireshark**: A network protocol analyzer that allows you to capture and analyze network traffic. By examining network packets, you can identify network bottlenecks, such as high latency, packet loss, or congestion.
   o **NetFlow Analyzer**: A tool that provides insights into network traffic and bandwidth usage, helping to identify bottlenecks in network-heavy applications.

USING PROFILING DATA

Once profiling tools have been used to collect performance data, the next step is to analyze that data to identify where improvements can be made. This often involves:

- **Identifying Hotspots**: Areas of code that consume disproportionate amounts of time or resources.

- **Analyzing Call Graphs**: Visual representations of function calls to see which functions are invoked most frequently or take the longest to execute.
- **Looking for Inefficiencies**: Inefficient memory usage, excessive disk I/O, or suboptimal algorithms that can be optimized.

8.3 Code Optimization Techniques

Code optimization is the process of improving the efficiency of software by making it run faster, consume less memory, or use fewer system resources. Here are several strategies to optimize code:

1. EFFICIENT ALGORITHMS

- **Algorithm Optimization**: The most significant improvements in performance often come from optimizing the algorithm. For instance, choosing an efficient sorting algorithm (like quicksort or mergesort) over a less efficient one (like bubble sort) can drastically reduce execution time.
- **Big-O Notation**: Understanding the time and space complexity of your algorithms using **Big-O notation** helps you assess how well they scale as the size of input data increases.

2. LOOP OPTIMIZATION

Loops are often a source of inefficiencies in code. Techniques to optimize loops include:

- **Unrolling Loops**: This involves reducing the number of iterations by performing multiple operations in one loop iteration. Loop unrolling can reduce overhead, especially in critical performance paths.
- **Avoiding Unnecessary Computations**: Avoid recalculating the same value multiple times inside loops. Store the result of a calculation in a variable and reuse it.

3. MEMORY OPTIMIZATION

- **Data Locality**: Arrange your data structures to optimize **cache locality**. The CPU cache is much faster than main memory, so grouping related data together in memory can reduce cache misses and speed up processing.
- **Minimize Memory Allocations**: Dynamically allocating memory can be slow. Where possible, allocate memory once and reuse it. Avoid frequent allocations and deallocations in performance-critical parts of your program.
- **Use Efficient Data Structures**: Choose data structures that suit your use case. For example, hash tables provide fast lookups, but arrays or linked lists may be more suitable for certain tasks.

4. PARALLELIZATION AND CONCURRENCY

Taking advantage of multiple CPU cores can significantly boost performance, especially for computationally intensive tasks. Techniques include:

- **Multithreading**: Splitting a task into smaller, independent threads that can run simultaneously.
- **Vectorization**: Using SIMD (Single Instruction, Multiple Data) instructions, which allow the CPU to process multiple data points in a single operation.
- **Distributed Computing**: Using multiple machines to distribute tasks and data across a network.

Since I/O operations can be slow, optimizing I/O access is critical for performance:

- **Batch Processing**: Grouping I/O operations together to minimize the overhead of initiating I/O requests.
- **Asynchronous I/O**: Using non-blocking I/O to prevent the program from waiting for I/O operations to complete before moving on to the next task.
- **Buffering**: Using buffers to store data temporarily before writing it to disk or sending it over a network can reduce the number of I/O operations.

8.4 Real-World Applications: Performance Tuning in Server Farms and High-Performance Computing

1. PERFORMANCE TUNING IN SERVER FARMS

In server farms (or data centers), performance tuning is critical to ensure that the systems can handle large-scale workloads. Server farms often deal with large volumes of data, many simultaneous requests, and the need to scale resources efficiently. Performance tuning techniques in server farms include:

- **Load Balancing**: Distributing requests across multiple servers to prevent any one server from becoming overloaded.
- **Cache Optimization**: Caching frequently accessed data closer to the user, reducing the need for repeated data retrieval from the database or backend servers.

- **Database Optimization**: Tuning database queries, indexing, and using database replication techniques to ensure fast data retrieval.

In high-performance computing (HPC) environments, performance tuning becomes even more important. HPC systems are often used for scientific simulations, machine learning, and other computationally intensive tasks. Optimizing these systems involves:

- **Efficient Use of Parallelism**: Distributing computational tasks across thousands of processors to maximize throughput.
- **Memory Hierarchy Optimization**: Ensuring that the system's memory hierarchy (L1, L2, L3 caches) is used effectively to minimize memory latency and maximize bandwidth.
- **Network Optimization**: Ensuring fast communication between nodes in a distributed system, which is crucial for applications that require massive parallelism and data sharing.

8.5 Hands-On Project: Optimize an Assembly Program for Speed

In this project, we will optimize a simple **assembly program** for speed. We will start with a basic program that performs a computational task (like calculating the sum of an array) and then apply various optimization techniques to make it run faster.

STEP 1: WRITE A BASIC PROGRAM

Let's begin with a simple program that sums an array of numbers.

asm

```
section .data
    numbers db 1, 2, 3, 4, 5    ; Array of numbers
    length equ 5                ; Length of the array

section .text
    global _start

_start:
    mov ecx, 0      ; Counter for array index
    mov ebx, 0      ; Sum variable

sum_loop:
    cmp ecx, length     ; Compare index with array
length
    je end_sum          ; If index == length, end the
loop
    add bl, [numbers + ecx]   ; Add current number to
sum
    inc ecx                   ; Increment index
    jmp sum_loop              ; Repeat the loop

end_sum:
    ; The sum is in the BL register
    mov eax, 1          ; Exit the program
    int 0x80
```

STEP 2: IDENTIFY BOTTLENECKS

Use profiling tools like **gProfiler** or **Intel VTune** to analyze the performance of the code. We might find that the loop is a performance bottleneck because it repeatedly accesses memory to fetch array elements.

We can optimize the program by:

- **Unrolling the loop** to reduce the overhead of checking the loop condition and jumping back.
- **Reducing memory access** by loading the data into registers and performing the calculation with registers instead of memory.

```asm
_start:
    mov eax, [numbers]          ; Load first 4 numbers into eax
    add eax, [numbers + 4]      ; Add the next 4 numbers
    add eax, [numbers + 8]
    add eax, [numbers + 12]
    ; Now eax holds the sum of the numbers
```

By reducing the number of memory accesses and using registers for computation, we significantly speed up the program.

After optimizing the code, run the program again and measure the performance improvements. You should see a significant decrease in the time it takes to execute the program, especially if you scale the array size.

Conclusion

In this chapter, we introduced the concept of **performance tuning**, a crucial practice for improving system efficiency. We discussed how to identify **bottlenecks** using profiling tools, and the various techniques for **code optimization**, such as improving algorithm efficiency, optimizing loops, reducing memory access, and leveraging parallelism.

We also explored how performance tuning is applied in **real-world scenarios**, such as server farms and **high-performance computing (HPC)** systems. Through the hands-on project, we learned how to optimize an **assembly program** for speed, applying real-world optimization strategies to improve system performance.

Chapter 9: Advanced Performance Tuning: Parallelism and Concurrency

OBJECTIVE

In this chapter, we will explore **advanced performance tuning techniques**, specifically focusing on **parallelism** and **concurrency**. As systems evolve and become more complex, optimizing performance involves not only making better use of hardware resources but also ensuring that software is designed to handle multiple tasks at the same time. **Parallel computing** and **multi-core systems** are the keys to this optimization, enabling software to run faster and more efficiently by distributing tasks across multiple processing units. By the end of this chapter, you'll understand the difference between parallelism and concurrency, learn how to write **assembly code for multi-threaded environments**, and implement a **parallel algorithm in assembly** to experience these concepts firsthand.

9.1 Understanding Parallel Processing and Multi-Core Systems

At the heart of **modern computing**, parallel processing and **multi-core systems** are essential to achieving high performance. The world has shifted from single-core processors, which could only handle one task at a time, to multi-core processors that can handle multiple tasks simultaneously. Let's explore how this works.

WHAT IS PARALLEL PROCESSING?

Parallel processing is the simultaneous execution of multiple tasks or processes. It is achieved by dividing a program or task into smaller, independent sub-tasks that can be executed concurrently across multiple processing units, such as CPU cores. **Parallelism** allows for faster computation because each core in a multi-core CPU can handle a different part of the workload, reducing the time it takes to complete the overall task.

- **Data Parallelism**: The same operation is applied to different pieces of data simultaneously. For example, adding elements from two arrays at the same time across multiple cores.
- **Task Parallelism**: Different tasks are performed simultaneously on different cores. For example, one core handles reading input while another handles computation and another manages output.

MULTI-CORE SYSTEMS

A **multi-core system** refers to a computer with a CPU that has multiple cores. Each core is capable of executing its own instruction stream, allowing for the parallel execution of instructions. Modern processors commonly feature **dual-core**, **quad-core**, or **octa-core** CPUs, which enable multiple instructions to be processed at once.

In multi-core systems, the CPU can execute **multiple threads** (smaller units of a process) concurrently, making better use of the system's resources and improving overall performance. However, not all software is designed to take advantage of multi-core systems, which is where parallel programming comes into play.

9.2 Concurrency vs. Parallelism: What's the Difference?

It's important to distinguish between **concurrency** and **parallelism** because, while they are related concepts, they are not the same. Both play a crucial role in optimizing system performance, but they are used in different contexts and ways.

CONCURRENCY

Concurrency refers to the ability of a system to manage multiple tasks or processes at once, even if they are not actually executing simultaneously. In other words, concurrency allows multiple tasks to make progress without necessarily completing all at once. The system can switch between tasks, providing the illusion of simultaneous execution, even though it might be executing them one at a time, quickly switching between them.

- **Example of Concurrency**: A program that handles multiple user inputs, reads data from a file, and performs calculations, all while appearing to operate simultaneously. It does this by rapidly switching between tasks using a **single core** or **multiple cores**, but the tasks themselves might not run at the exact same time.

PARALLELISM

Parallelism, on the other hand, involves actually executing multiple tasks at the same time, typically on **multiple processing units** (e.g., CPU cores or even different machines in a distributed system). Parallelism can only occur if there are enough physical resources (like CPU cores) to handle the simultaneous execution.

- **Example of Parallelism**: A program that splits a large dataset into chunks and processes each chunk on a different core. Each core is executing its own task simultaneously, resulting in a significant reduction in processing time.

KEY DIFFERENCE

- **Concurrency** is about managing multiple tasks in a way that makes progress on each one, even if they aren't executed at the same time.
- **Parallelism** is about executing multiple tasks simultaneously, leveraging the hardware's resources.

In short, **concurrency** deals with structure and coordination of tasks, while **parallelism** is about the actual execution of those tasks in parallel.

9.3 Writing Assembly for Multi-Threaded Environments

Writing **assembly code for multi-threaded environments** requires an understanding of how modern processors handle multiple threads and how to use them effectively. Assembly programming in multi-core environments can be more challenging because the programmer needs to manually manage the synchronization of tasks and ensure that threads do not interfere with one another.

THREADS AND CONTEXT SWITCHING

A **thread** is the smallest unit of execution within a process. Modern operating systems and processors allow multiple threads to be executed concurrently or in parallel. In assembly language, managing threads means managing the **thread context**, which includes registers, memory, and program counter.

- **Context Switching**: In a multi-core system, the CPU can switch between threads on the same core. This process is known as **context switching**. The operating system typically handles this by saving the state of a running thread and loading the state of the next thread.

In assembly, working with multi-threaded environments means using **system calls** or **processor-specific instructions** to create, manage, and synchronize threads.

ATOMIC OPERATIONS AND SYNCHRONIZATION

In a multi-threaded environment, threads often need to share data. Without proper synchronization, this can lead to **race conditions**, where the outcome depends on the sequence of thread execution, leading to unpredictable results.

Atomic operations are low-level operations that are guaranteed to complete without interruption. These operations ensure that a thread's changes to data are immediately visible to other threads without interference.

Common atomic operations include:

- **Compare-and-swap**: Used to check if a value matches a certain condition before modifying it.
- **Test-and-set**: Sets a value to true and returns the previous value, useful for locking mechanisms.

Synchronization primitives like **mutexes** and **semaphores** are used in higher-level programming languages, but in assembly, you can implement synchronization manually using atomic instructions or memory barriers.

9.4 Hands-On Project: Implement a Parallel Algorithm in Assembly

Now that we've covered the theoretical background, let's put our knowledge into practice by writing a parallel algorithm in assembly. We'll implement a simple **parallel summation algorithm** that splits an array into multiple chunks and calculates the sum using multiple threads.

STEP 1: DEFINE THE PROBLEM

We'll start by writing a parallel algorithm to sum the values in an array. Let's assume the array is large and we want to use multiple threads to sum different portions of the array in parallel.

1. Split the array into chunks, with each chunk assigned to a different core.
2. Each thread (running on its own core) sums its chunk of the array.
3. The final step is to combine the results from each thread into one total sum.

STEP 2: SETUP THE ENVIRONMENT

For this project, we'll be working with an **x86** processor in **real mode**. We'll write the assembly code using **NASM** (Netwide Assembler) and simulate a multi-threaded environment.

Since real-mode assembly doesn't have built-in multi-threading, we will simulate it by dividing the work manually. On a true multi-core system, the operating system would handle the scheduling of threads across multiple cores.

Here's a simplified version of how we can divide the summation task into chunks:

```asm
section .data
    numbers db 1, 2, 3, 4, 5, 6, 7, 8, 9, 10  ; Array
of numbers
    length equ 10                             ;
Length of the array
    result db 0                               ;
Result of the summation

section .text
    global _start

_start:
    ; Initialize registers
    mov ecx, 0          ; Array index
    mov ebx, 0          ; Sum for the first chunk

    ; First thread summation (simulate with ECX loop)
sum_loop_1:
    cmp ecx, 5          ; Limit first thread to the
first 5 elements
    je end_sum_1
    add ebx, [numbers + ecx]
    inc ecx
    jmp sum_loop_1

end_sum_1:
    ; Store the result of first chunk in the result
    mov [result], ebx
```

```
    ; Second thread summation (simulate with ECX
loop)
    mov ecx, 5          ; Reset index for second chunk
    mov ebx, 0          ; Reset sum for the second
chunk

sum_loop_2:
    cmp ecx, 10         ; Limit second thread to the
last 5 elements
    je end_sum_2
    add ebx, [numbers + ecx]
    inc ecx
    jmp sum_loop_2

end_sum_2:
    ; Add the result of second chunk to the total
result
    add [result], ebx

    ; Exit
    mov eax, 1          ; Exit system call
    int 0x80
```

STEP 4: EXPLANATION OF THE CODE

- We first initialize the **ECX** register to track the array index, and the **EBX** register to hold the sum for each chunk.
- The program divides the array into two chunks:
  - The first chunk sums the first 5 numbers.
  - The second chunk sums the remaining numbers.
- The sum for each chunk is stored in the **result** variable.
- After summing both chunks, the program exits.

This simulation manually divides the work between two "threads" using a loop. In a true multi-core environment, each thread would run concurrently on different cores, executing the same logic independently.

Now that the parallel summation algorithm is implemented, test the program to ensure it produces the correct result. In a real multi-core system, each thread would be able to run independently, providing a performance boost. To simulate performance improvements, try increasing the array size and analyze the time it takes for the algorithm to run.

To optimize this code for speed:

- **Unroll loops** to reduce the overhead of loop control.
- **Use registers** more efficiently to minimize memory access.
- Consider further **parallelization** if the task can be divided into more chunks, allowing even more cores to be utilized.

9.5 Conclusion

In this chapter, we explored **advanced performance tuning** techniques by delving into **parallelism** and **concurrency**. We learned about **multi-core systems** and how they enable true parallel processing, significantly improving performance for computationally intensive tasks. We also clarified the difference between concurrency (managing multiple tasks) and parallelism (simultaneously executing multiple tasks), emphasizing the importance of both concepts in modern computing.

Through the **hands-on project**, we implemented a **parallel summation algorithm** in assembly language, simulating multi-threading on a single-core system. This project allowed us to experience parallelism in action and understand the challenges and benefits of writing parallel programs.

Chapter 10: Advanced Hardware Control: Interfacing with Custom Hardware

OBJECTIVE

In this chapter, we will delve into **advanced techniques** for controlling **custom hardware devices** and **peripherals**. Understanding how to interface with external hardware is a critical skill for anyone working with **embedded systems**, custom electronics, or hardware-oriented applications. We will cover how to interact with hardware through **General Purpose Input/Output (GPIO)** pins, how to program **embedded systems in assembly**, and tackle some **practical challenges** faced in hardware control. To solidify your understanding, we will complete a **hands-on project** where you will write assembly code to control an **LED display**—a common but essential task in embedded systems.

10.1 Interfacing with External Hardware Through GPIO Pins

WHAT ARE GPIO PINS?

General Purpose Input/Output (GPIO) pins are digital pins on a microcontroller or computer that can be programmed to either input data (from external devices) or output data (to control external devices). GPIO pins are a fundamental tool in embedded systems and can be used to interact with a wide range of hardware devices, such as LEDs, buttons, sensors, motors, and displays.

GPIO pins can be configured as:

- **Input**: When configured as input, the GPIO pin can read data from external devices. For example, it can detect the state of a button (pressed or not).
- **Output**: When configured as output, the GPIO pin can send data to external devices, such as lighting up an LED or activating a relay.

Each GPIO pin is connected to a physical pad on the microcontroller or processor, and it can be controlled programmatically. The state of a GPIO pin is typically represented as a **digital signal**, meaning it can either be **high** (1) or **low** (0). A high state typically means **voltage is present**, and a low state means **no voltage**.

GPIO PIN MODES AND CONTROL

To work with GPIO pins, you need to configure them in software to determine their behavior. Most microcontrollers provide access to GPIO through control registers, which define the pin's behavior. For example:

- **Direction Register**: Defines whether the pin is an input or output.
- **Data Register**: Holds the value of the pin (high or low).
- **Control Register**: Configures additional features like pull-up resistors or alternate functions (e.g., PWM or analog input).

By toggling these registers, you can read from or write to GPIO pins to control connected hardware.

Working with GPIO in Assembly

To control GPIO pins in **assembly language,** we need to interact with the microcontroller's hardware registers. This process varies depending on the specific microcontroller or processor you're working with (such as **ARM, AVR,** or **PIC**), but the basic principles are the same.

For instance, consider the following steps for controlling a GPIO pin on an **AVR** microcontroller:

1. **Set the pin direction** (input or output) by writing to the **DDRx register** (Data Direction Register).
2. **Write to the data register** (PORTx) to set the pin high or low if it is an output.
3. **Read from the data register** (PINx) if the pin is configured as an input.

Here's an example in AVR assembly that sets a GPIO pin as output and turns it on (high):

asm

```
; Set PINB0 as output
ldi r16, (1<<PB0)        ; Load value to set PB0 as
output (bit 0 high)
out DDRB, r16            ; Write to DDRB to set pin
direction

; Set PINB0 high
ldi r16, (1<<PB0)        ; Load value to set PB0 high
out PORTB, r16           ; Write to PORTB to set pin
high
```

This simple assembly code snippet demonstrates how to configure a GPIO pin for output and then set it high, turning on an external device like an LED.

10.2 Programming Embedded Systems in Assembly

Embedded systems are specialized computer systems that do not look like typical computers. They are often small, resource-constrained devices designed for a specific purpose, such as controlling a thermostat, a robotic arm, or an LED display. Programming embedded systems in assembly gives you precise control over hardware resources, but it also comes with unique challenges.

WHY USE ASSEMBLY FOR EMBEDDED SYSTEMS?

Assembly language allows for low-level programming that provides the ability to directly control hardware. For embedded systems, this is crucial because:

- **Efficiency**: Assembly code is highly optimized and uses minimal system resources, which is essential in resource-constrained environments.
- **Real-time control**: Assembly language provides fine-grained control over timing and hardware interactions, which is vital for real-time applications.
- **Minimal overhead**: Assembly is free of the abstractions and overhead that come with high-level programming languages, making it ideal for low-power or small devices.

UNDERSTANDING EMBEDDED SYSTEM HARDWARE

Before you can write assembly for an embedded system, you must understand the hardware you're working with. Embedded systems often use microcontrollers or microprocessors, and each comes with its own set of **peripherals** (e.g., timers, ADCs, I/O ports) and **special registers** that control them.

For example, consider a **microcontroller** with the following typical components:

- **GPIO pins** for interacting with external devices.
- **Timers** for creating time delays or scheduling events.
- **Analog-to-Digital Converters (ADC)** for reading analog sensors.
- **UART (Universal Asynchronous Receiver/Transmitter)** for serial communication with external devices.

Programming these peripherals in assembly often involves writing directly to **special function registers** that control their operation.

ASSEMBLY AND INTERRUPTS IN EMBEDDED SYSTEMS

One of the key features of embedded systems is the use of **interrupts**. An interrupt is a mechanism that allows the CPU to temporarily stop executing its current task and jump to a special routine (called an **interrupt service routine**, or ISR) to handle an event, such as a timer expiring or a button press.

Writing assembly code for interrupt-driven systems typically involves:

1. **Enabling interrupts**: Setting control registers to enable the interrupt in question.
2. **Writing the ISR**: Writing the code that will run when the interrupt occurs.
3. **Returning from the ISR**: Using special instructions to return control to the interrupted task.

10.3 Practical Challenges in Hardware Control

When working with hardware, there are several practical challenges to consider, including:

1. TIMING AND SYNCHRONIZATION

Many hardware devices require precise timing to function correctly. For example, when controlling an LED display, you need to ensure that data is sent to the display at the correct intervals. Handling this in assembly can be difficult because it requires low-level control of **timers** and **interrupts** to keep everything synchronized.

2. POWER MANAGEMENT

Embedded systems often run on battery power, so managing power consumption is critical. In assembly, you can optimize power by controlling the **sleep modes** of peripherals and minimizing the CPU's workload when not needed.

3. DEBUGGING AND TESTING

Embedded systems can be challenging to debug because they often lack the rich debugging tools available in traditional programming environments. You may need to rely on **hardware debuggers**, **oscilloscopes**, and **serial output** to observe how the system behaves during runtime.

10.4 Hands-On Project: Control an LED Display Using Assembly

In this project, we will write assembly code to control a **7-segment LED display** connected to an embedded system. A 7-segment display is a common output device used to show numerical values (or letters) using seven individual LEDs arranged in a specific pattern.

STEP 1: UNDERSTANDING THE 7-SEGMENT DISPLAY

A **7-segment LED display** has seven individual LEDs arranged in a figure-eight pattern, where each segment can be turned on or off to form numbers (and some letters). Here's how the segments are usually labeled:

```lua
    -- a --
   |       |
  f|       |b
   |       |
    -- g --
   |       |
  e|       |c
   |       |
    -- d --
```

Each of the seven segments is controlled individually. To display a number, you need to turn on specific segments. For example:

- To display the number 0, all segments except g (the middle) should be on.

STEP 2: CONNECT THE DISPLAY TO THE MICROCONTROLLER

You can connect the 7-segment display to the microcontroller's **GPIO pins,** with each pin controlling one segment of the display. For simplicity, let's assume that each GPIO pin controls one segment directly.

For example:

- `PORTA0` could control segment `a`
- `PORTA1` could control segment `b`
- And so on...

STEP 3: WRITE THE ASSEMBLY CODE

Here is a simple assembly program to display a number on the 7-segment display. The number will be displayed by turning on the appropriate segments.

```asm
asm

section .data
    ; Define segment patterns for numbers 0-9
    ; Each byte corresponds to one digit. Bits
represent segments a-g
    ; 0 = off, 1 = on
    segments db 0x3F, 0x06, 0x5B, 0x4F, 0x66, 0x6D,
0x7D, 0x07, 0x7F, 0x6F

section .text
    global _start

_start:
    ; Initialize the microcontroller GPIO pins (e.g.,
PORTA as output)
    ; Assuming registers for configuring ports are
already set

    ; Display number 5 on the 7-segment display
```

```asm
    mov al, 5              ; Load the number 5 (to
display '5') into AL
    mov bl, [segments + al] ; Get the segment pattern
for 5
    out 0xPORTA, bl       ; Output the pattern to PORTA
(control the GPIO pins)

    ; Halt the program
    mov eax, 1            ; Exit system call
    int 0x80
```

In this code:

- The segments array defines the bit patterns for displaying digits 0-9.
- The number 5 is loaded into the AL register, and the corresponding bit pattern for 5 is retrieved from the segments array.
- The pattern is sent to PORTA, which controls the 7-segment display. Each bit in bl corresponds to a segment, turning the appropriate segments on or off to display the number.

STEP 4: TEST THE PROGRAM

Once the assembly code is written, assemble and run it on a microcontroller or simulator with a 7-segment display connected to it. Observe the display to see if the correct number is shown. You can modify the code to display different numbers by changing the value of al.

STEP 5: TROUBLESHOOT AND OPTIMIZE

If the display isn't working as expected, check the connections between the microcontroller and the 7-segment display. Ensure the correct GPIO pins are used for each segment and that the microcontroller is configured properly.

10.5 Conclusion

In this chapter, we covered the advanced techniques used to control **custom hardware devices** and **peripherals**, focusing on **GPIO** pins, **assembly programming for embedded systems**, and the **practical challenges** of hardware control. We learned how to interface with external hardware, including the crucial steps of configuring GPIO pins, reading from and writing to memory-mapped I/O registers, and controlling devices like LEDs and displays.

Through the **hands-on project**, we implemented a simple program in assembly to control a **7-segment LED display**. This project helped reinforce the concepts of GPIO pin control, timing, and assembly programming for embedded systems.

Chapter 11: Assembly Language in Real-Time Systems

In this chapter, we'll explore the role of **assembly language** in **real-time systems**, where **timing** is absolutely crucial. Real-time systems are designed to perform tasks within strict timing constraints. This means that the system must meet deadlines for task execution, often in environments where delays can result in failure or catastrophic consequences. We will discuss what makes a system **real-time**, how to write **time-critical assembly programs**, manage **task scheduling**, and handle **interrupts** efficiently. Additionally, we will have a hands-on project where you'll create a **real-time control system** using assembly language to experience how low-level programming interacts with real-time constraints.

11.1 What Makes a System "Real-Time"?

A **real-time system** is a computer system designed to respond to input or events within a guaranteed time frame. This is in contrast to general-purpose computing systems, where response time is typically not as critical. In real-time systems, **time constraints** play a key role in ensuring the system meets its operational goals.

HARD VS. SOFT REAL-TIME SYSTEMS

There are two main categories of real-time systems:

1. **Hard Real-Time Systems**:
   - These systems have **strict timing constraints** that must be met. If a task misses its deadline, the system fails. This could result in catastrophic consequences, particularly in safety-critical applications like medical devices, aerospace systems, and automotive safety systems.
   - **Example**: A **pacemaker** must deliver electrical impulses to the heart at precise intervals, or the patient's life could be in danger. If the pacemaker misses a beat, the system fails.
2. **Soft Real-Time Systems**:
   - Soft real-time systems are more flexible. Missing a deadline does not cause system failure, but it may degrade performance or user experience. In these systems, timing is important but not absolutely critical.
   - **Example: Video streaming applications** such as Netflix or YouTube. A slight delay in data transmission may cause a momentary buffer, but it does not result in the failure of the entire system.

THE IMPORTANCE OF TIMELINESS IN REAL-TIME SYSTEMS

In real-time systems, **task deadlines** are crucial, and tasks must be completed within the time frame specified by the system's requirements. This leads to the need for precise control over hardware and software resources. Real-time systems often involve **interrupts, time-triggered execution**, and **predictable task scheduling** to ensure the system meets its deadlines.

11.2 Writing Time-Critical Assembly Programs

When programming for real-time systems, **assembly language** is often preferred due to its efficiency, low overhead, and the control it provides over system resources. In time-critical systems, every cycle counts, and assembly allows you to minimize unnecessary operations and gain full control over the execution of instructions.

WHY ASSEMBLY FOR REAL-TIME SYSTEMS?

Assembly language allows programmers to write highly optimized code that interacts directly with the hardware. This is essential in **real-time systems** because:

- **Minimal Overhead**: Assembly allows for minimal system overhead by eliminating the abstraction layers found in higher-level programming languages.
- **Fine Control**: Assembly gives you full control over hardware peripherals, memory, and registers, enabling precise timing and coordination.
- **Predictable Execution**: With assembly, you can ensure that the system performs only the necessary tasks, with no extra delays introduced by the operating system or runtime environment.

KEY CONSIDERATIONS FOR TIME-CRITICAL ASSEMBLY PROGRAMMING

1. **Instruction Timing**:
    - In assembly, the **execution time of each instruction** is predictable. This is crucial in real-time systems because knowing how long an instruction will take allows you to accurately plan task execution.
    - **Example**: A **NOP (No Operation)** instruction may take one clock cycle, while an **ADD** instruction might take several cycles. Assembly allows you to count and manage cycles to ensure tasks complete on time.
2. **Minimizing Latency**:

- o **Latency** is the time between when an event occurs and when the system responds. In real-time systems, minimizing latency is vital. Assembly allows you to optimize code paths and avoid delays caused by higher-level abstractions like memory management and garbage collection.
3. **Task Isolation and Prioritization**:
   - o **Task isolation** ensures that one task does not interfere with another. In assembly, this can be achieved through careful management of registers and memory.
   - o **Task prioritization** allows high-priority tasks to execute before low-priority ones. Real-time systems often involve a **priority-based scheduling system**, which can be implemented in assembly by checking conditions in the **status registers** or implementing **interrupt-based task switching**.

11.3 Task Scheduling and Interrupt Handling

One of the most critical components of real-time systems is **task scheduling**. Task scheduling determines when and how tasks are executed within a system, ensuring that tasks meet their deadlines. In real-time systems, this involves both **time-triggered** and **event-triggered** scheduling techniques.

TIME-TRIGGERED VS. EVENT-TRIGGERED SCHEDULING

1. **Time-Triggered Scheduling**:
   - o In time-triggered systems, tasks are executed at specific times or after defined intervals. The system's clock controls the scheduling of tasks, and each task

is assigned a specific time slice or time window to run.

- o **Example:** In embedded control systems for automotive applications, tasks like **sensor polling** or **engine control** are scheduled at fixed intervals.

2. **Event-Triggered Scheduling:**
   - o In event-triggered systems, tasks are executed in response to an event, such as a **hardware interrupt**. The CPU temporarily stops executing the current task and runs the interrupt service routine (ISR) when a particular event occurs.
   - o **Example:** An automotive airbag system uses event-triggered scheduling. The system responds to signals from crash sensors to deploy the airbags instantly when needed.

INTERRUPT HANDLING IN REAL-TIME SYSTEMS

In real-time systems, **interrupts** are used to handle asynchronous events. An interrupt signals the CPU to stop its current execution and handle a high-priority event (like a sensor reading or a timer expiring).

Interrupts are used to ensure that time-critical tasks get immediate attention from the CPU. These interrupts can be **hardware interrupts** (generated by external devices like sensors or timers) or **software interrupts** (generated by the software to request system services).

- **Interrupt Service Routine (ISR):** An ISR is a small piece of code executed in response to an interrupt. It should be as short and efficient as possible to avoid delaying other time-sensitive tasks.
- **Interrupt Latency:** This refers to the time between when an interrupt is generated and when the ISR starts executing. In

real-time systems, interrupt latency must be minimized to ensure timely responses.

- **Nested Interrupts**: In some cases, interrupts can be nested, meaning one interrupt can preempt another interrupt. This allows high-priority interrupts to preempt lower-priority ones.

USING ASSEMBLY FOR INTERRUPT HANDLING

In assembly language, handling interrupts typically involves:

1. **Enabling Interrupts**: The interrupt system must be enabled by setting the appropriate bits in the processor's interrupt control registers.
2. **Writing the ISR**: The ISR is written in assembly to quickly process the interrupt and perform the necessary actions.
3. **Context Switching**: The CPU saves the current state of the registers when an interrupt occurs and restores it when the ISR is complete, allowing the system to resume the interrupted task seamlessly.

11.4 Hands-On Project: Create a Real-Time Control System in Assembly

Now that we've covered the theory, let's implement a real-time control system using assembly language. In this project, we will simulate a simple **real-time control system** for a robotic arm. The robotic arm needs to respond to sensor input (simulated by a button press) and move to specific positions based on the input.

STEP 1: DEFINE THE PROBLEM

The robotic arm has three positions: low, medium, and high. We will use a button to simulate an external trigger (e.g., a sensor). When the button is pressed:

- The arm will move to the low position.
- When the button is pressed again, the arm will move to the medium position.
- When pressed again, the arm will move to the high position.

The control system needs to respond to the button press within **a few milliseconds** to ensure smooth operation.

STEP 2: SET UP THE HARDWARE

For this example, we'll assume that the button is connected to a **GPIO pin** and that the robotic arm's position is controlled by a **motor** connected to another set of GPIO pins. We will write the assembly code to control the hardware:

1. **GPIO Pin for Button**: We will configure a GPIO pin as input to read the button press.
2. **GPIO Pins for Motor**: We will use three GPIO pins to control the motor's position (low, medium, and high).

STEP 3: WRITE THE ASSEMBLY CODE

The program will:

- Continuously monitor the button state.
- When the button is pressed, the program will toggle the robotic arm's position by setting the appropriate GPIO pins high or low.

```asm
asm

section .data
    low_position db 0x01 ; Motor control bit for low
position
    medium_position db 0x02 ; Motor control bit for
medium position
    high_position db 0x04 ; Motor control bit for
high position

section .bss
    button_state resb 1

section .text
    global _start

_start:
    ; Configure button GPIO pin as input
    ; Configure motor control pins as output
(assumed)

    ; Main loop
main_loop:
    ; Read button press (polling)
    mov al, [button_state] ; Read button state into
AL
    test al, al             ; Test if the button is
pressed (assumes 1 = pressed)
    jz main_loop            ; If not pressed, keep
checking

    ; Change arm position based on current position
    ; Toggle motor position: Low -> Medium -> High ->
Low
    cmp byte [low_position], 0
    je set_medium
    cmp byte [medium_position], 0
    je set_high
    cmp byte [high_position], 0
    je set_low

set_medium:
    ; Set motor to medium position
    mov al, [medium_position]
```

```
    ; Set GPIO pins accordingly (send signal to
motor)
    ; Perform some delay to simulate action
    ; Jump back to main loop
    jmp main_loop

set_high:
    ; Set motor to high position
    mov al, [high_position]
    ; Set GPIO pins accordingly
    ; Perform some delay
    jmp main_loop

set_low:
    ; Set motor to low position
    mov al, [low_position]
    ; Set GPIO pins accordingly
    ; Perform some delay
    jmp main_loop
```

In this code:

- We check the button state in a continuous loop.
- When the button is pressed, we toggle the motor's position by setting different GPIO pins high.
- The motor control logic switches between **low**, **medium**, and **high** positions based on the current state.

STEP 4: IMPLEMENT TIMING AND DELAYS

In real-time systems, timing is essential. We need to ensure that each state change happens in a controlled manner. You can use **timing loops** or a **hardware timer** to manage the time spent in each position. Here's an example of a simple delay loop in assembly:

```
asm

delay:
    ; Perform a time delay (simple loop)
    mov cx, 50000          ; Set the delay time
```

```
delay_loop:
    dec cx
    jnz delay_loop
    ret
```

This delay function will help create a timed gap between each motor action, ensuring the system reacts in real-time but without overshooting or causing unnecessary jitter.

STEP 5: TEST AND OPTIMIZE

Once the system is built and the code is written, test the functionality. The button should toggle the arm's position between low, medium, and high. You can optimize the delay times, adjust the motor control logic, and ensure that the system's response time is fast enough to meet the requirements of the task.

11.5 Conclusion

In this chapter, we learned about the **role of assembly language** in **real-time systems**, where timing and precision are critical. We discussed what makes a system "real-time", the differences between **hard** and **soft real-time systems**, and how assembly language is ideal for programming time-critical systems due to its low overhead and precise control over hardware.

We also covered key concepts such as **task scheduling, interrupt handling**, and **timing** in assembly, which are essential for real-time system development. Through the **hands-on project**, we implemented a simple **real-time control system** using assembly language, simulating the control of a robotic arm using GPIO pins and interrupts.

Chapter 12: Microservices Architecture and Assembly Language

OBJECTIVE

In this chapter, we will bridge the gap between **traditional system programming** and **modern microservices architecture**, particularly from the perspective of low-level **assembly language**. Microservices architecture has become the go-to approach for building scalable and maintainable systems. However, most microservices tutorials focus on high-level languages and abstract away low-level hardware interactions. By understanding how **system-level programming** can interface with microservices, we can optimize certain aspects of microservices, particularly in performance-critical applications. We will discuss the basics of microservices, how **system-level programming** (in assembly) can complement microservices, and how to design efficient microservices in low-level assembly. Finally, we will develop a **hands-on project** to create a simple microservice that communicates with hardware.

12.1 What is Microservices Architecture?

Microservices architecture is an approach to software design where a system is broken down into smaller, self-contained **services** that operate independently. Each service is responsible for a single, specific business function and can be developed, deployed, and scaled independently of the others.

KEY CHARACTERISTICS OF MICROSERVICES:

1. **Independence**:
   - Each microservice is a **standalone unit** that has its own logic and operates independently. Services communicate with each other through lightweight mechanisms like HTTP or messaging queues.
2. **Distributed**:
   - Microservices run independently and often across multiple machines or containers. They are usually deployed on cloud platforms and communicate over networks.
3. **Autonomy**:
   - Each service has its own **data store** and manages its own database. This means services are loosely coupled and can operate without depending on each other's databases.
4. **Scalability**:
   - Since microservices are independent, they can be scaled individually. If one service experiences high traffic, only that service needs to be scaled up, making the system more **resource-efficient**.
5. **Resilience**:
   - Microservices can be more resilient than monolithic applications because failure in one service does not necessarily mean the failure of the entire system. Each service has its own fault tolerance mechanisms.
6. **Continuous Deployment**:
   - Microservices allow for **continuous integration** and **continuous deployment (CI/CD)**, enabling independent updates and versioning of services.

Microservices architecture is widely used in building large-scale applications like:

- **E-commerce websites** (e.g., Amazon, eBay)
- **Streaming platforms** (e.g., Netflix, Spotify)
- **Financial systems** (e.g., banking applications)
- **Cloud-based applications** (e.g., AWS Lambda)

Each of these examples uses microservices to break down complex functionality into smaller, manageable pieces that can evolve independently over time.

12.2 How System-Level Programming Interfaces with Microservices

At first glance, **system-level programming** (such as assembly language) might seem far removed from **microservices architecture**, which is typically associated with high-level programming languages like **Java**, **Python**, or **Go**. However, understanding the low-level details of system performance and **hardware interaction** can provide a **competitive advantage** when optimizing certain aspects of microservices.

SYSTEM-LEVEL PROGRAMMING IN MICROSERVICES:

1. **Interfacing with Hardware**:
   - Microservices often rely on hardware, either locally or through networked systems, for their operations. **System-level programming** can be used to

interface directly with hardware or manage hardware resources in real-time.

- o **Example**: If a microservice needs to read sensor data from a hardware device, a low-level assembly language program could handle the hardware interface, providing the necessary data to a higher-level microservice via a network API.

2. **Optimizing Performance**:
   - o While high-level languages provide **convenience**, they also add overhead in terms of memory management, garbage collection, and CPU cycles. **Assembly language** allows for **fine-tuned optimization**, especially for performance-critical applications like high-frequency trading or real-time processing.
   - o **Example**: If a microservice needs to process large amounts of data in real-time, using assembly to optimize certain tasks (such as compression, encryption, or parsing) can greatly improve the overall system performance.

3. **Resource Efficiency**:
   - o **Assembly** allows developers to write highly efficient code that consumes minimal CPU and memory. In a microservices architecture, where resources are often limited (especially in **containerized** or **serverless** environments), this efficiency can reduce operational costs.

4. **Embedded Systems Integration**:
   - o Many microservices interact with **embedded systems**—devices like sensors, controllers, or IoT devices. Low-level programming is crucial in these environments to control hardware accurately, which then feeds data into the microservices layer.
   - o **Example**: A microservice controlling a robot might rely on assembly code to interface with sensors and actuators, ensuring precise timing and control over hardware.

12.3 Designing Efficient Microservices with Low-Level Assembly

Although most microservices are written in high-level languages, low-level programming such as **assembly** can still play a role in microservices, especially in resource-constrained environments. By carefully designing microservices with assembly in mind, developers can optimize certain aspects of system performance.

1. MINIMIZING RESOURCE USAGE

Microservices are often run in **containerized environments** (e.g., Docker, Kubernetes), and efficient use of resources is essential to maximizing their performance. In a containerized environment, resource constraints such as memory, CPU, and storage are common. Writing **assembly code** for low-level tasks can reduce the resource usage of specific components of a service.

- **Example:** An embedded system service that interfaces with an IoT device may use assembly to read data from sensors with minimal memory overhead, ensuring that the rest of the service (running in a container) uses as few resources as possible.

2. HIGH-PERFORMANCE DATA PROCESSING

Microservices dealing with large-scale data often need to process information in real-time, such as in video streaming, financial trading, or sensor networks. Low-level programming with assembly can significantly **optimize data processing** tasks by:

- **Direct memory manipulation**: Manipulating large datasets directly in memory without the overhead of higher-level data structures.
- **Minimizing branching**: Writing code that avoids unnecessary branching and uses **CPU caches** efficiently to speed up data access.
- **Example**: If you are building a service that processes high-frequency trading data, optimizing the core processing loop using assembly can help ensure that the service can handle thousands of transactions per second with minimal latency.

3. WRITING PERFORMANCE-CRITICAL MICROSERVICES IN ASSEMBLY

When writing **time-sensitive operations** in assembly for microservices, you will be controlling how tasks are scheduled, how interrupts are handled, and how data is moved between hardware and software. Aspects such as the **CPU cycle**, **memory cache**, and **timing constraints** need to be meticulously managed to meet microservice performance goals.

- **Example**: In a microservice controlling real-time data for a **smart manufacturing plant**, using assembly for low-level control of actuators and sensors ensures that the microservice meets its strict time constraints, such as ensuring machines receive commands within milliseconds.

12.4 Hands-On Project: Create a Microservice that Communicates with Hardware

Let's now dive into a hands-on project where we will implement a simple **microservice** that communicates with hardware. In this example, we will create a microservice that reads data from a

temperature sensor (simulated by hardware through GPIO) and sends this data to a RESTful API endpoint for other services to consume. The assembly code will handle the hardware interface, and a higher-level language will manage the API.

STEP 1: SET UP THE HARDWARE

We'll simulate hardware communication using **GPIO pins** connected to a temperature sensor. The sensor sends data as a simple 8-bit number representing the temperature, which the microservice reads and processes. In this example, we will assume an **ARM-based microcontroller** with an operating system that supports **RESTful API** communication.

STEP 2: WRITE ASSEMBLY CODE TO READ DATA FROM GPIO

We will write assembly code that reads the temperature data from the GPIO pin connected to the sensor. This involves setting the GPIO pin as an **input** and then reading the value.

```asm
asm

section .data
    sensor_data db 0             ; Placeholder for
sensor data

section .bss
    gpio_register resb 1         ; Reserve a byte for
GPIO input

section .text
    global _start

_start:
    ; Set the GPIO pin as input (assuming
microcontroller control registers)
```

```
    ; This would typically involve writing to control
registers

    ; Read the value from the GPIO pin (simulating
sensor data)
    mov al, [gpio_register]      ; Read the GPIO pin
value into AL
    mov [sensor_data], al        ; Store it in the
sensor_data variable

    ; Perform some processing (e.g., scaling or
converting sensor data)
    ; For simplicity, we're just passing the data
along

    ; Send the data to the higher-level service (not
shown here in assembly)
    ; In real systems, we could use interrupts or a
communication protocol to transmit the data
    ret
```

This simple assembly code reads a value from the GPIO register and stores it in a variable. This data can be further processed, formatted, or transmitted to a higher-level microservice or API.

STEP 3: WRITE THE HIGHER-LEVEL MICROSERVICE

Once we have the hardware interface in place, we can write a higher-level service in a language like **Python** or **Go** to handle the data coming from the assembly program and expose it via an API.

Here's a **Python Flask** example of the microservice that exposes the temperature data through a RESTful API:

```python
python

from flask import Flask, jsonify
import os

app = Flask(__name__)
```

```
@app.route('/temperature', methods=['GET'])
def get_temperature():
    # Read the temperature data (this would be
interfaced with hardware or assembly)
    sensor_data = os.popen("cat
/sys/class/gpio/gpio17/value").read()
    temperature = int(sensor_data)  # Convert the
data to an integer
    return jsonify({'temperature': temperature})

if __name__ == '__main__':
    app.run(debug=True, host='0.0.0.0', port=5000)
```

This simple microservice listens on port 5000 and exposes a
/temperature endpoint that provides the current temperature
data. It reads the value from the GPIO (or assembly code) and
returns it as JSON.

STEP 4: INTEGRATING THE MICROSERVICE

Finally, the assembly code reads data from the hardware sensor,
which is then processed by the Python microservice. To integrate
them, you can use inter-process communication (IPC), shared
memory, or direct system calls to pass data between the assembly
code and the microservice.

12.5 Conclusion

In this chapter, we explored how **assembly language** and
microservices architecture can work together to create high-
performance, hardware-interfacing microservices. We covered the
basics of **microservices**, the role of **assembly** in optimizing

hardware interactions, and how low-level programming can be integrated into modern software architectures.

Through the **hands-on project**, we learned how to create a **microservice that communicates with hardware**, bridging the gap between system-level programming and modern microservices. This process involves writing assembly to interact with hardware (via GPIO), creating a higher-level service to manage data, and exposing the data via an API for external use.

Chapter 13: Debugging and Troubleshooting Low-Level Code

OBJECTIVE

In this chapter, we will focus on the techniques used for **debugging** and **troubleshooting** low-level code, particularly in **assembly language** and **machine code**. Unlike high-level programming languages, where debugging tools like IDEs offer sophisticated features (breakpoints, watches, etc.), low-level programming often requires a deeper understanding of the hardware and a more hands-on approach to debugging. We will discuss **common bugs** in assembly programs, the **tools and techniques** used for debugging machine code, and **real-world debugging scenarios** that will give you the skills to resolve issues effectively. We will finish with a **hands-on project** where you will debug a simple assembly program that contains an error.

13.1 Common Bugs in Assembly Programs

Assembly programs are particularly challenging to debug because they operate **closer to the hardware**, and small mistakes can have profound effects on program behavior. Even a single misplaced instruction can cause issues ranging from **incorrect program output** to **system crashes**. Understanding common bugs in assembly programming can help you identify and solve problems more quickly.

1. Incorrect Memory Access

One of the most common issues in assembly programs is incorrect memory access. In assembly, you deal directly with memory addresses, and mistakes here can lead to **segmentation faults** or **unexpected behavior**. Common problems include:

- **Accessing uninitialized memory**: Trying to read from a memory location that hasn't been initialized yet.
- **Out-of-bounds memory access**: Trying to access memory that's beyond the allocated space for an array or buffer, potentially corrupting data.

Example:

```asm
mov al, [ebx]   ; Attempting to read from an
uninitialized memory address stored in ebx
```

To fix this, ensure that memory addresses are correctly initialized and always check bounds before accessing arrays or buffers.

2. Stack Mismanagement

Assembly code often involves pushing and popping values onto the **stack**. Improper management of the stack can lead to errors like **stack overflows**, **stack underflows**, and **incorrect function return values**.

- **Stack overflow**: If too many values are pushed onto the stack without popping them off, it can overflow the stack and overwrite critical memory.
- **Stack underflow**: If values are popped from the stack without being pushed first, the program may try to access data that doesn't exist.

Example:

```asm
push eax   ; Pushes a value to the stack
pop ebx    ; Pops the value to ebx (if not pushed
before, this will cause an issue)
```

To avoid stack issues, always ensure that the number of **pushes** and **pops** are balanced, and check the **stack pointer** register (`esp` in x86) during execution to ensure it remains within bounds.

3. INCORRECT REGISTER USAGE

In assembly, registers are small, fast storage locations used to hold intermediate data. However, incorrect usage of registers can result in bugs. Common mistakes include:

- **Overwriting a register** that still holds important data.
- **Using the wrong register** for the intended purpose, which can lead to unexpected behavior in complex algorithms.

Example:

```asm
mov eax, 10   ; Correctly storing a value in eax
add eax, ebx  ; Incorrectly using eax instead of
another register for the calculation
```

Always keep track of which data is stored in each register, especially when multiple operations are performed in the same function.

4. Infinite Loops and Incorrect Loop Control

Loops in assembly are often used to repeat operations until a condition is met. However, if the loop termination condition is incorrect or if the loop control registers are mismanaged, the program can get stuck in an **infinite loop**.

Example:

```asm

mov ecx, 5          ; Set loop counter to 5
loop_start:
dec ecx             ; Decrement ecx
jnz loop_start      ; Jump to loop_start if ecx is not
zero (infinite loop if ecx doesn't reach 0)
```

To avoid infinite loops, double-check your **loop control logic** and ensure that the **counter register** reaches the intended termination condition.

5. Incorrect Flag Management

In assembly, the **status flags** (like **zero flag (ZF)**, **carry flag (CF)**, **sign flag (SF)**) are used to store the results of arithmetic and logical operations. Incorrect flag manipulation can result in erroneous decisions or logic flow.

- **Example:** After performing a comparison (cmp), the **zero flag** will indicate if two values are equal. If you forget to check the flag after the comparison, you might make an incorrect decision.

13.2 Tools and Techniques for Debugging Machine Code

Debugging low-level code can be challenging because you often need to understand how your program interacts with the hardware at the **binary level**. Fortunately, there are several tools and techniques available to make this process easier.

1. DEBUGGING WITH DISASSEMBLERS

A **disassembler** is a tool that takes machine code (binary) and converts it into human-readable assembly code. This allows you to analyze the compiled program, understand what instructions it is executing, and identify potential bugs.

- **Example**: Tools like **IDA Pro** or **Ghidra** can be used to disassemble a compiled program and analyze its assembly code.

Using a disassembler is useful when you have machine code (e.g., from a firmware image) but no access to the original source code.

2. USING A DEBUGGER

A **debugger** is a tool that allows you to execute a program step-by-step, inspect the state of registers, memory, and flags, and even modify them during runtime. Some common debuggers for low-level programs include:

- **GDB** (GNU Debugger): A popular debugger for Linux systems. It allows you to step through assembly code, inspect memory, and set breakpoints.
- **OllyDbg**: A debugger for Windows applications that helps in debugging machine code and assembly.

Basic Debugging Workflow:

1. **Set Breakpoints**: Pause execution at specific points in the program.
2. **Step Through Code**: Execute the program one instruction at a time to observe how registers and memory change.
3. **Inspect Registers and Memory**: View the contents of registers and memory addresses to verify the correctness of the program.

3. PRINT DEBUGGING

In low-level programming, print statements might not be as straightforward as in high-level languages. However, you can use **system calls** or **interrupts** to print data to a console or serial port for debugging purposes.

- **Example (Linux)**: To print a value to the console, you could use a **syscall** to write to stdout.

asm

```
mov eax, 4       ; Syscall for write
mov ebx, 1       ; File descriptor for stdout
mov ecx, msg     ; Message to print
mov edx, 13      ; Message length
int 0x80         ; Make the syscall
```

This technique is invaluable when debugging low-level code, especially when you can't use a high-level debugger to inspect variables.

4. USING EMULATORS AND SIMULATORS

Sometimes, debugging hardware-related issues requires simulating the hardware itself. **Emulators** and **simulators** allow you to run low-level code in an environment where you can test how your program interacts with the hardware without having direct access to it.

- **Example: QEMU** is an emulator that can simulate hardware architectures and run assembly code, allowing you to test your code before deploying it on actual hardware.
- **Example: Proteus** can simulate microcontroller circuits and embedded programs, making it ideal for debugging embedded assembly programs.

5. MEMORY INSPECTION TOOLS

Tools like **Valgrind** (for memory-related bugs in C/C++) and **memcheck** allow you to inspect memory usage and identify **memory leaks, segmentation faults**, and other issues that might arise from incorrect memory access in low-level code.

13.3 Real-World Debugging Scenarios

Let's now look at a few real-world debugging scenarios to better understand how these tools and techniques can be applied to solve problems in assembly programs.

SCENARIO 1: INTERRUPT HANDLING GONE WRONG

Imagine you're working on an embedded system where you're using interrupts to handle external events (e.g., a button press). However, the system doesn't respond to button presses correctly.

1. **Problem**: The interrupt is not being triggered as expected.
2. **Step 1**: Use a debugger to step through the interrupt setup code to ensure that the interrupt enable bit is set correctly.

3. **Step 2**: Check the interrupt vector table to ensure that the correct **ISR** (Interrupt Service Routine) is being executed.
4. **Step 3**: Use an emulator or print statements to confirm that the correct hardware interrupt is being fired.

By stepping through the assembly code and checking the system's response to interrupts, you'll pinpoint where the issue lies (e.g., a missing instruction or incorrect flag).

Scenario 2: Stack Overflow in Embedded Systems

You're developing firmware for a simple microcontroller-based system, and the program crashes intermittently. After examining the crash logs, you suspect a **stack overflow**.

1. **Problem**: The stack pointer is overwriting important data due to excessive function calls.
2. **Step 1**: Use a debugger to inspect the **stack pointer (SP)** and **base pointer (BP)** registers at the point of the crash.
3. **Step 2**: Check if the function calls are properly nested and whether there's a mismatch between **pushes** and **pops** to/from the stack.
4. **Step 3**: Look for **infinite recursion** or **excessive memory usage** in certain functions.

In this case, using the debugger to inspect the stack and registers will help pinpoint where the overflow is happening, allowing you to fix the issue by adjusting the function calls or optimizing the stack usage.

Scenario 3: Incorrect Memory Access

You're writing a low-level program that interacts with hardware through memory-mapped I/O. However, certain memory locations are returning garbage values, leading to incorrect operation.

1. **Problem**: Incorrect memory address or uninitialized memory access.
2. **Step 1**: Use a disassembler to review the generated machine code and ensure that memory addresses are correctly aligned and calculated.
3. **Step 2**: Set breakpoints before memory access instructions to inspect the address being accessed.
4. **Step 3**: Use print debugging to output the address being accessed and check if it's within the expected range.

By carefully analyzing the assembly code and using memory inspection tools, you can track down incorrect memory accesses and resolve the issue by fixing the address calculations or initialization.

13.4 Hands-On Project: Debug an Assembly Program with an Error

In this hands-on project, we'll work through a simple assembly program with an intentional error. Your goal is to debug and troubleshoot the issue using the techniques and tools discussed in this chapter.

STEP 1: THE PROBLEM

Let's assume we have an assembly program designed to calculate the sum of an array. However, the program is producing incorrect results. Here's the code:

```
asm

section .data
    numbers db 10, 20, 30, 40, 50  ; Array of numbers
```

```
    sum db 0                        ; Variable to store
sum

section .text
    global _start

_start:
    ; Initialize registers
    mov ecx, 5          ; Number of elements in array
    mov ebx, 0          ; Initialize sum to 0
    mov esi, numbers    ; Point to the start of the
array

loop_start:
    add ebx, [esi]      ; Add the current number to sum
    inc esi             ; Move to the next element
    dec ecx             ; Decrement loop counter
    jnz loop_start      ; Repeat until all elements are
processed

    ; Store the sum in memory (incorrect address
here)
    mov [sum], ebx      ; Store sum into sum
(incorrectly)

    ; Exit the program
    mov eax, 1          ; Exit system call
    int 0x80
```

STEP 2: DIAGNOSIS

The program should sum the values in the numbers array and store
the result in sum. However, the sum is not being stored correctly.

1. **Problem**: The program stores the result of the summation
   into the wrong memory address. The issue is that the
   variable sum is declared as a **byte** (db), but the result (ebx) is
   a **32-bit** register. This can lead to incorrect behavior.
2. **Step 3: Use a Debugger**

Step through the program in a debugger to inspect the value in the `ebx` register. Check if it matches the expected sum of $10 + 20 + 30 + 40 + 50 = 150$.

<u>STEP 4: FIX THE ERROR</u>

The fix is simple: change `sum db 0` to `sum dd 0`, which allocates **4 bytes** (enough space for the 32-bit sum).

asm

```
section .data
    numbers db 10, 20, 30, 40, 50  ; Array of numbers
    sum dd 0                        ; Allocate 4 bytes
for the sum
```

<u>STEP 5: RE-TEST AND VERIFY</u>

Run the program again, and use debugging tools or print statements to verify that the sum is now correctly calculated and stored.

13.5 Conclusion

In this chapter, we've learned essential techniques for **debugging** and **troubleshooting** low-level code, particularly in **assembly language**. Debugging assembly code requires a deep understanding of the system's hardware and memory architecture. We covered **common bugs** in assembly programs, such as **incorrect memory access**, **stack mismanagement**, and **incorrect flag usage**, and we discussed various **tools and techniques** for debugging machine code, including **disassemblers**, **debuggers**, and **print debugging**.

We also explored **real-world debugging scenarios**, like interrupt handling errors, stack overflows, and memory access issues, and used practical tools to resolve them. Finally, in the **hands-on project**, we debugged an assembly program with an error, allowing us to apply the techniques discussed in a real-world scenario.

Chapter 14: Integrating Assembly with High-Level Languages

In this chapter, we'll explore how **assembly language** can be integrated with **high-level languages** like **C**, **C++**, or **Python** to optimize performance-critical parts of a program. While high-level languages are great for writing robust and maintainable code, there are situations where assembly language can provide significant performance improvements. We'll discuss when and why to use assembly alongside high-level languages, how to interface between them, and demonstrate a real-world example of using assembly in performance-critical sections, such as **web servers**. To help you put theory into practice, we'll have a **hands-on project** where we write a high-performance algorithm using both **C** and **assembly** to get the best of both worlds.

14.1 When and Why to Use Assembly Alongside C, C++, or Python

High-level languages like **C**, **C++**, and **Python** are ideal for writing general-purpose code because they abstract away much of the complexity of the hardware and provide extensive libraries and frameworks. However, for certain applications where **performance** and **efficiency** are critical, relying solely on high-level languages may not yield the desired results. This is where **assembly language** comes into play.

1. **Performance Optimization**:
   Assembly allows for **low-level control** of hardware resources, enabling you to write highly optimized code for specific tasks. In high-performance applications, even small optimizations at the assembly level can lead to substantial improvements.
2. **Time-Critical Code**:
   When timing is critical, such as in **real-time systems**, **video encoding**, or **cryptography**, assembly can be used to implement **time-sensitive algorithms** that run as quickly as possible. High-level languages might introduce **latency** or **overhead** that could affect system performance.
3. **Hardware-Specific Optimizations**:
   Some processors and architectures provide **specialized instructions** (e.g., SIMD, vector operations) that can be leveraged in assembly but are often difficult to access directly from high-level languages. Writing assembly gives you the ability to use these instructions effectively.
4. **Minimal Resource Usage**:
   Embedded systems, **IoT devices**, or **low-power devices** often have very limited resources. In such environments, assembly allows for **tight control** over memory usage and CPU cycles, which is essential for efficient operation.
5. **Legacy Systems**:
   Many legacy systems were programmed in assembly or require low-level optimizations. Even when working with modern high-level languages, you might need to integrate assembly to interface with these systems or optimize existing code.

1. **Optimizing Critical Sections**: In most cases, you don't need to write an entire application in assembly. Instead, you can write the **performance-critical parts** in assembly and leave the rest of the application in a high-level language.
   - **Example**: If you're building a **web server**, the core logic (e.g., processing requests, managing connections) might be implemented in **C or C++**, but tasks like **data encryption** or **compression** could be written in assembly for speed.
2. **Performance Bottlenecks**: When profiling your application reveals specific **bottlenecks** that limit performance, you can write **assembly code** to address those specific bottlenecks while keeping the rest of the system written in a higher-level language.
3. **Hardware Access**: Some tasks, like **interfacing with specialized hardware** (e.g., graphics cards, sensors, or custom devices), require direct control over registers and memory. Assembly can help you access and manage hardware resources more efficiently than a high-level language.
4. **Inline Assembly**: Some compilers (e.g., **GCC, Clang**) allow you to **embed assembly code** directly within your C or C++ programs using **inline assembly**. This allows you to write critical parts of the code in assembly without needing to separate the assembly and high-level code into different files.

14.2 Interfacing Assembly with High-Level Languages

Interfacing assembly with high-level languages like **C** or **C++** requires understanding how the two languages interact with each other, especially regarding **function calls**, **register usage**, and **memory management**. Here are some key concepts when integrating assembly with high-level languages:

1. Calling Conventions

A **calling convention** defines how functions receive parameters, return values, and how the stack is managed. When you call a function from **C** or **C++**, you usually don't need to worry about the details of the calling convention, as the compiler handles it. However, when mixing assembly with high-level code, it's essential to respect the calling convention.

The most common calling conventions are:

- **cdecl (C Declaration)**: The caller cleans up the stack after the function call. This is used in C and C++ compilers for **x86** systems.
- **stdcall (Standard Call)**: The callee cleans up the stack. Common in Windows API functions.
- **fastcall**: The first few arguments are passed in registers, speeding up function calls.

When writing assembly code that calls a C function or is called by a C function, you need to ensure that the registers and the stack are managed according to the calling convention being used.

2. Register Usage

In assembly, registers hold data temporarily for processing. In high-level languages, the compiler uses registers for variable storage, but in assembly, you have direct control over which registers are used for what purpose.

When interfacing assembly with C or C++, you need to be aware of which registers are preserved across function calls. For instance, in **cdecl**, the **callee** is expected to preserve the registers `ebx`, `esi`, and `edi`, while the caller cleans up the stack.

You should avoid using the same registers for different purposes between assembly and high-level code unless you explicitly save and restore them.

3. PASSING PARAMETERS

Parameters can be passed to functions via registers or the stack. When calling a function from assembly or calling assembly from a high-level language, it's essential to know how parameters are passed.

- **In C/C++**, parameters are often passed via the stack or in registers (depending on the calling convention).
- **In assembly**, parameters are typically pushed onto the stack before making a function call, and the return value is usually placed in a register (`eax` for 32-bit systems in x86).

You must ensure the correct passing of parameters, especially when working with **64-bit systems** (where registers like `rdi`, `rsi`, `rdx`, etc., are used for the first few parameters).

4. HANDLING RETURN VALUES

In C or C++, functions return values through specific registers (for example, `eax` for integer types in **x86**). When writing assembly that interacts with C functions, you should store the return value in the appropriate register.

14.3 Real-World Example: Performance-Critical Sections in Web Servers

In many real-world applications, certain parts of the program require high performance to meet strict timing or load requirements. A **web server** is a great example of a system that benefits from **performance tuning**, as it needs to handle many requests concurrently while minimizing response time.

PERFORMANCE BOTTLENECKS IN WEB SERVERS

While most web server logic is implemented in high-level languages like **C** or **C++**, certain tasks—such as **data encryption**, **compression**, or **hashing**—are performance-critical and may require low-level optimizations.

- **Encryption**: When handling sensitive data, web servers often use encryption algorithms like **AES** (Advanced Encryption Standard) or **RSA** for secure communication. These algorithms involve numerous mathematical operations that can benefit from low-level optimizations.
- **Compression**: Web servers often need to compress large files (e.g., images, videos, or HTML pages) before serving them. Compression algorithms like **gzip** or **LZ77** can be optimized with assembly to reduce processing time.

OPTIMIZING CRYPTOGRAPHIC FUNCTIONS WITH ASSEMBLY

For example, consider the **AES encryption algorithm**. AES involves many rounds of substitution and permutation, which can be computationally intensive. By implementing these operations in assembly, you can achieve significant performance gains over the high-level versions of the algorithm.

Here's a simple overview of how an **AES encryption** function could be optimized in assembly:

1. **SubBytes**: The substitution step replaces each byte with another based on a pre-defined substitution table.
2. **ShiftRows**: This step shifts the rows of the state array.
3. **MixColumns**: This step mixes the columns of the state array to provide diffusion.

Each of these steps can be optimized in assembly by directly using CPU instructions that perform the operations faster than high-level loops or function calls.

INTEGRATING THE ASSEMBLY CODE INTO A C-BASED WEB SERVER

Let's say you are writing a web server in **C** that needs to use AES encryption. Instead of writing the encryption code in C, you could implement the critical parts of the AES algorithm in assembly for speed and then call the assembly function from C.

c

```
extern "C" {
    void aes_encrypt(uint8_t *input, uint8_t
*output);
}

int main() {
    uint8_t input[16] = { ... }; // 128-bit block of
data
    uint8_t output[16];          // Output buffer for
encrypted data
    aes_encrypt(input, output); // Call the assembly
function for encryption
    return 0;
}
```

Here, the `aes_encrypt` function is written in assembly, and the C program calls it just like a normal C function.

14.4 Hands-On Project: Write a High-Performance Algorithm Using Both C and Assembly

In this project, we'll combine **C** and **assembly** to optimize a **matrix multiplication** algorithm. Matrix multiplication is a performance-critical operation, often used in scientific computing, machine learning, and data processing.

STEP 1: WRITE A BASIC MATRIX MULTIPLICATION IN C

Here's a simple implementation of matrix multiplication in **C**:

c

```c
#include <stdio.h>

void matrix_multiply(int A[3][3], int B[3][3], int C[3][3]) {
    for (int i = 0; i < 3; i++) {
        for (int j = 0; j < 3; j++) {
            C[i][j] = 0;
            for (int k = 0; k < 3; k++) {
                C[i][j] += A[i][k] * B[k][j];
            }
        }
    }
}

int main() {
    int A[3][3] = {{1, 2, 3}, {4, 5, 6}, {7, 8, 9}};
    int B[3][3] = {{9, 8, 7}, {6, 5, 4}, {3, 2, 1}};
    int C[3][3];
```

```
matrix_multiply(A, B, C);

for (int i = 0; i < 3; i++) {
    for (int j = 0; j < 3; j++) {
        printf("%d ", C[i][j]);
    }
    printf("\n");
}

return 0;
}
```

This basic implementation is sufficient for small matrices, but it can be inefficient for large matrices due to the nested loops.

STEP 2: OPTIMIZE THE ALGORITHM WITH ASSEMBLY

We will now optimize the innermost loop of the matrix multiplication using assembly. The assembly code will directly access the elements of the matrices and perform the multiplication faster than the high-level C code.

Here's an optimized version using inline assembly in **GCC**:

c

```
void matrix_multiply_optimized(int A[3][3], int
B[3][3], int C[3][3]) {
    for (int i = 0; i < 3; i++) {
        for (int j = 0; j < 3; j++) {
            C[i][j] = 0;
            for (int k = 0; k < 3; k++) {
                __asm__ (
                    "movl %[a], %%eax;"      // Load
A[i][k] into eax
                    "movl %[b], %%ebx;"      // Load
B[k][j] into ebx
                    "imull %%ebx, %%eax;"    //
Multiply A[i][k] * B[k][j]
```

```
                    "addl %%eax, %[c];"        // Add
the result to C[i][j]
                    : [c] "+r" (C[i][j])      //
Output: C[i][j] is updated
                    : [a] "r" (A[i][k]), [b] "r"
(B[k][j]) // Inputs: A[i][k], B[k][j]
                    : "%eax", "%ebx"          //
Clobbered registers
                );
            }
        }
    }
}
```

This assembly code optimizes the multiplication by directly using the `imull` instruction, which multiplies two integers and stores the result in a register, avoiding the need for multiple arithmetic operations in C.

STEP 3: COMPARE PERFORMANCE

Now, you can benchmark the performance of the original C implementation and the optimized version. Depending on the size of the matrices and the platform you're running on, you should see significant performance improvements with the assembly optimization.

14.5 Conclusion

In this chapter, we explored the integration of **assembly language** with **high-level languages** like **C**, **C++**, and **Python** to optimize performance. We learned when and why assembly should be used alongside these languages, how to interface between them, and the value of using assembly for **performance-critical** sections of applications.

Through the **hands-on project**, we optimized a **matrix multiplication algorithm** by writing performance-critical sections in assembly, demonstrating the power of combining high-level abstractions with low-level optimizations. This approach allows developers to get the best of both worlds: ease of development with high-level languages and maximum performance with assembly.

Chapter 15: Future Trends and Advanced Topics in System Architecture

OBJECTIVE

As we move deeper into the 21st century, system architecture continues to evolve with the emergence of **new technologies** and **innovations**. In this chapter, we'll take a forward-looking approach to the field of system architecture, exploring the **future role of assembly and machine language**, the potential impact of **quantum computing**, and the increasing importance of **hardware/software co-design**. These trends are shaping the future of computing, and understanding them will be crucial for anyone interested in the cutting-edge advancements of system architecture. We'll also end the chapter with a **hands-on project**, where we'll explore a **simple quantum computing algorithm**, helping to bring the theoretical concepts to life.

15.1 The Role of Assembly and Machine Language in Future Computing

For many, assembly language and machine language are seen as relics of the past, often associated with outdated computing systems or niche applications. However, as computing systems become more complex and performance demands increase, the **role of low-level languages** will continue to be critical in ensuring that systems can perform efficiently, even in next-generation computing environments.

1. CONTINUED RELEVANCE OF LOW-LEVEL PROGRAMMING

Even as high-level programming languages dominate development, **assembly language** and **machine language** remain foundational to the design and optimization of modern computing systems. These low-level languages are essential for:

- **Optimizing performance**: As computing workloads grow in complexity, especially with tasks like **data processing, AI computations**, or **real-time systems,** low-level control will be needed to squeeze out every last bit of performance from hardware.
- **Real-time and embedded systems**: Assembly language will continue to be critical for programming **real-time systems** and **embedded devices**, where performance, low power consumption, and precise control over hardware are essential.
- **Hardware-specific optimizations**: Many future computing architectures will introduce custom **instruction sets**, requiring low-level programmers to write optimized code that leverages these unique instructions, especially in high-performance computing (HPC), AI, and machine learning.

2. MACHINE LANGUAGE IN NEW ARCHITECTURES

As **specialized hardware** like **Graphics Processing Units (GPUs)**, **Field-Programmable Gate Arrays (FPGAs)**, and **Application-Specific Integrated Circuits (ASICs)** become more widely used, machine-level programming will be required to take full advantage of their capabilities. These devices often come with **unique instruction sets** or hardware accelerators, and utilizing them efficiently demands low-level programming.

Example: GPUs, commonly used for parallel processing in **machine learning**, operate using **SIMD (Single Instruction, Multiple Data)** instructions. Low-level programming techniques will be needed to optimize these operations, especially as more general-purpose programming languages like Python use these devices.

3. ASSEMBLY IN FUTURE COMPUTING TECHNOLOGIES

As emerging technologies like **quantum computing** begin to shape the computing landscape, low-level languages like assembly and machine code will be necessary to interface with new hardware architectures. For example, **quantum assembly languages** will be needed to write programs for **quantum processors**, similar to how assembly language is currently used to interface with classical processors.

Quantum Computing is fundamentally different from classical computing, and as quantum computers become more powerful, there will be a growing need for assembly-level programming to control quantum hardware at the lowest level.

15.2 Quantum Computing and Its Impact on Low-Level Programming

Quantum computing is one of the most exciting and revolutionary technologies on the horizon. It has the potential to solve problems that are currently intractable for classical computers, such as **cryptography**, **complex simulations**, and **optimization problems**. But quantum computing brings with it a new set of challenges and opportunities for low-level programming.

1. WHAT IS QUANTUM COMPUTING?

Quantum computing leverages the principles of **quantum mechanics**, which govern the behavior of matter at very small scales (such as atoms and photons). The most critical concept in quantum computing is the **quantum bit (qubit)**, which differs from a classical bit in that it can represent both **0 and 1 simultaneously** due to the **principle of superposition**. This property enables quantum computers to perform many calculations in parallel.

Another key concept is **entanglement**, which allows qubits to be correlated in ways that classical bits cannot. This means that quantum computers can solve certain types of problems exponentially faster than classical computers.

2. LOW-LEVEL PROGRAMMING FOR QUANTUM COMPUTERS

Unlike classical computers, which are based on **binary logic** and perform computations using well-established instruction sets (like **x86** or **ARM**), quantum computers require a completely different approach to programming. **Quantum assembly languages** are emerging as the tool for writing low-level code to control quantum processors.

Some quantum programming languages and tools already exist, such as **QASM (Quantum Assembly Language)** and **Q#** by Microsoft. These languages allow programmers to control quantum circuits, including operations like **quantum gates** and **measurements**, at a low level.

Low-level quantum programming will involve tasks such as:

- **Setting up quantum circuits**: Designing and implementing sequences of quantum operations (gates) that manipulate qubits.
- **Error correction**: Quantum computers are highly susceptible to noise and errors, so low-level programming will also need to address error-correction techniques to ensure reliable calculations.
- **Interfacing with classical hardware**: Quantum computers are often used alongside classical systems, and low-level programming will be necessary to interface quantum processors with classical processors, sensors, and storage devices.

3. QUANTUM ALGORITHMS AND THEIR ROLE IN LOW-LEVEL PROGRAMMING

Quantum algorithms like **Shor's algorithm** for factoring large numbers and **Grover's algorithm** for searching unsorted databases provide exponential speedups over their classical counterparts. Implementing these algorithms efficiently will require a deep understanding of the quantum hardware and low-level control of quantum gates, circuits, and qubits.

For example, when implementing Shor's algorithm, low-level programming might involve constructing **modular exponentiation circuits** to process the large numbers involved in the factorization process. These quantum operations are quite different from classical operations, and they require careful optimization at the assembly level.

15.3 The Growing Importance of Hardware/Software Co-Design

In the future of system architecture, **hardware/software co-design** will become increasingly important. Co-design is a methodology that integrates hardware and software development to create more efficient and specialized systems. Instead of designing hardware and software separately, co-design allows both to be developed together to achieve better performance and resource utilization.

1. THE NEED FOR CO-DESIGN

As computing systems become more complex and specialized, particularly with the rise of **AI**, **edge computing**, **5G**, and **quantum computing**, the boundaries between hardware and software are blurring. Traditional approaches to system design treat hardware and software as separate entities, but this is no longer sufficient to meet the demands of modern systems.

- **Example:** In **AI** and **machine learning**, hardware accelerators like **TPUs (Tensor Processing Units)** or **FPGAs** are optimized to execute certain mathematical operations more efficiently than general-purpose CPUs. In these cases, the hardware must be tightly integrated with the software to maximize performance.
- **Example:** In **edge computing**, where computational resources are distributed across multiple devices in real-time environments, optimizing hardware and software for low power consumption and minimal latency is crucial. The software needs to work in tandem with the underlying hardware to ensure timely decision-making and fast response times.

2. HARDWARE/SOFTWARE CO-DESIGN IN ASSEMBLY PROGRAMMING

Assembly language plays a critical role in hardware/software co-design. When writing low-level software to interface with hardware, assembly provides the precision needed to optimize performance and control hardware resources directly. In hardware/software co-design, assembly might be used for:

- **Optimizing communication between hardware and software**: Writing low-level drivers and control routines that handle data transfer between processors, memory, and peripherals.
- **Implementing specialized instructions**: Using assembly to take advantage of specialized hardware instructions or features like SIMD (Single Instruction, Multiple Data) operations in **vector processors** or quantum operations in quantum processors.

As hardware becomes more specialized, assembly language will remain essential for **fine-tuning** and ensuring that hardware and software work in harmony to achieve maximum efficiency.

3. CO-DESIGN IN QUANTUM AND CLASSICAL SYSTEMS

In the case of **quantum-classical hybrid systems**, hardware/software co-design will be crucial. A **quantum computer** might be used to solve part of a problem (e.g., quantum simulations, optimizations), while the **classical system** handles the majority of the task. Effective communication and synchronization between these two types of systems will require low-level programming skills to ensure seamless interaction.

15.4 Hands-On Project: Explore a Simple Quantum Computing Algorithm

Now that we've explored the theoretical underpinnings of **quantum computing**, let's dive into a **hands-on project** where we implement a simple quantum computing algorithm.

STEP 1: SET UP YOUR QUANTUM DEVELOPMENT ENVIRONMENT

To get started, we'll need access to a quantum computing framework. For this project, we'll use **Qiskit**, a popular open-source framework developed by IBM for quantum computing.

1. **Install Qiskit**: If you haven't already, install Qiskit using the following command:

   bash

   ```
   pip install qiskit
   ```

2. **Set up your IBM Q account**: Create a free account on IBM Q to access cloud-based quantum computers for running your programs.

STEP 2: CREATE A SIMPLE QUANTUM CIRCUIT

We'll implement a simple **quantum algorithm**: the **Quantum Coin Toss**. This algorithm involves creating a quantum circuit that initializes a qubit in a superposition state and then measures the qubit to simulate a coin toss.

Here's the Python code that creates the quantum circuit using **Qiskit**:

python

```python
from qiskit import QuantumCircuit, Aer, execute

# Create a quantum circuit with one qubit and one
classical bit
qc = QuantumCircuit(1, 1)

# Apply a Hadamard gate to create a superposition
qc.h(0)

# Measure the qubit and store the result in the
classical bit
qc.measure(0, 0)

# Use the Aer simulator to simulate the quantum
circuit
simulator = Aer.get_backend('qasm_simulator')

# Execute the circuit on the simulator
job = execute(qc, simulator, shots=1000)

# Get the result of the simulation
result = job.result()
counts = result.get_counts(qc)

# Print the result
print(f"Coin Toss Result: {counts}")
```

In this code:

- We create a **quantum circuit** with one qubit and one classical bit.
- A **Hadamard gate** is applied to the qubit, which creates a superposition state (the quantum equivalent of flipping a coin).
- The qubit is measured, and the result is stored in the classical bit.
- The **Aer simulator** is used to simulate the quantum circuit, and we execute the circuit 1,000 times to observe the result.

After running the program, you should see a distribution of results like `{'0': 502, '1': 498}`, meaning the quantum coin toss is roughly evenly split between heads (0) and tails (1), as expected in a fair coin toss.

The integration of quantum algorithms with classical systems is key to **quantum-classical hybrid computing**. For example, once the quantum part of the algorithm completes, you can take the result and feed it into a classical system for further processing, such as in optimization problems.

In a real-world scenario, you might use **quantum circuits** to perform complex tasks (like factorizing large numbers using **Shor's algorithm**) and then use classical systems to post-process the results.

15.5 Conclusion

In this chapter, we explored the **future trends** in system architecture, focusing on the emerging role of **assembly language**, **quantum computing**, and **hardware/software co-design**. We discussed how assembly language will continue to play a crucial role in performance-critical applications, even as modern architectures evolve. We also examined the **impact of quantum computing** on system design and the future of low-level programming in the quantum era.

By completing the **hands-on project**, we gained a practical understanding of how to implement and run a simple quantum algorithm using **Qiskit**. This project serves as a starting point for more complex quantum-classical systems and illustrates the intersection of quantum and classical computing.

As we move forward, the integration of quantum computing, low-level programming, and hardware/software co-design will shape the future of system architecture.

Conclusion: Your Path Forward in System Architecture

<u>OBJECTIVE</u>

As we reach the end of this book, it's important to reflect on the key skills we've covered and how they can be applied in the real world. The journey through **system architecture**, **low-level programming**, and **hardware/software co-design** has provided you with a strong foundation to take your technical knowledge to the next level. In this concluding chapter, we'll recap the essential concepts we've explored, provide resources to continue your learning journey, and guide you on how to apply your newfound skills in **real-world projects**. Finally, we'll challenge you with a **final project** that allows you to design your **own system architecture project from scratch**, putting everything you've learned into practice.

1. Recap of Skills Learned Throughout the Book

Throughout this book, we've covered a broad range of topics essential to understanding modern system architecture, low-level programming, and the integration of hardware and software. Here's a recap of the most important skills you've learned and how they contribute to a deeper understanding of system architecture:

1.1 Fundamentals of Assembly and Machine Language

We began by exploring the basics of **assembly language** and **machine code**, which are the building blocks of computer systems. These low-level languages allow you to interact directly with the hardware, giving you control over system resources such as memory, CPU registers, and input/output devices. Understanding these languages provides insight into how high-level programming languages work under the hood and enables you to optimize programs for performance.

Key Takeaways:

- Assembly language enables you to write efficient, hardware-specific code.
- Machine language is the lowest-level representation of code executed by the CPU.
- Understanding the architecture of a processor helps in designing optimized programs.

1.2 System-Level Programming and Architecture

We delved into **system architecture**, including how components like the **CPU**, **memory**, and **I/O systems** interact. You learned how **microarchitecture** and **system-level programming** come together to create efficient and high-performing systems. Understanding these concepts is critical for building or optimizing systems from the ground up.

Key Takeaways:

- System-level programming allows direct control over hardware resources.
- Microarchitecture plays a crucial role in performance.

- The interaction between memory, registers, and I/O is essential for designing efficient systems.

1.3 DEBUGGING AND TROUBLESHOOTING LOW-LEVEL CODE

One of the most important aspects of low-level programming is debugging. We covered how to identify and resolve common bugs in assembly code, including issues like **incorrect memory access**, **stack mismanagement**, and **infinite loops**. You also learned about various **tools** and **techniques** for debugging low-level code, such as **disassemblers**, **debuggers**, and **memory inspection tools**.

Key Takeaways:

- Debugging low-level code requires an understanding of the hardware and memory architecture.
- Tools like **GDB** and **IDA Pro** are invaluable for stepping through assembly code and identifying issues.
- **Memory management** and understanding the **stack** are crucial for error-free low-level programming.

1.4 INTEGRATING ASSEMBLY WITH HIGH-LEVEL LANGUAGES

In this section, we explored how **assembly language** can be integrated with high-level languages like **C**, **C++**, and **Python**. This integration is critical for optimizing performance in **performance-critical sections** of applications, such as web servers, cryptographic algorithms, and video processing. You learned about **calling conventions, register management**, and how to **interface** assembly with high-level code.

Key Takeaways:

- **Assembly** is used to optimize performance in specific parts of an application.
- Low-level programming skills can complement high-level languages by providing direct hardware access and minimizing overhead.
- Understanding how to interface assembly with high-level code improves your ability to design efficient systems.

1.5 QUANTUM COMPUTING AND ITS ROLE IN LOW-LEVEL PROGRAMMING

We explored the exciting world of **quantum computing**, focusing on how this new paradigm will change the way we think about computation. You learned about **quantum algorithms,** such as **Shor's algorithm** and **Grover's algorithm**, and how **quantum assembly languages** will play a crucial role in programming quantum computers. We also discussed how **quantum programming** intersects with traditional low-level programming.

Key Takeaways:

- Quantum computing introduces a new realm of computational possibilities.
- Quantum programming languages like **QASM** and **Q#** will be essential for writing low-level quantum code.
- The integration of **quantum and classical systems** will require a strong foundation in low-level programming.

1.6 PERFORMANCE TUNING AND REAL-TIME SYSTEMS

We covered how to optimize **system performance** using **parallelism** and **concurrency**, and how assembly language can be used to optimize time-critical code. You learned about **task scheduling**, **interrupt handling**, and how to write **time-sensitive assembly programs** for real-time systems. These techniques are essential when building systems that must meet strict deadlines or respond to events in real time.

Key Takeaways:

- **Performance tuning** is critical for systems that need to handle large-scale data or real-time processing.
- Assembly language provides the precision needed to optimize time-sensitive operations.
- **Interrupt handling** and **task scheduling** are key elements in designing real-time systems.

---

2. Resources for Continued Learning

While this book has provided a solid foundation in **system architecture** and **low-level programming**, the journey does not end here. The field of system architecture is constantly evolving, and continued learning is essential to staying up-to-date with new technologies, tools, and methodologies. Below are some resources that will help you deepen your understanding and continue your journey into advanced topics in system architecture and low-level programming:

2.1 BOOKS AND TEXTS

1. **"The Art of Computer Programming" by Donald E. Knuth**
   This is a comprehensive and essential text for anyone serious about low-level programming and algorithmic design. It covers topics ranging from basic data structures to advanced algorithms and optimizations.
2. **"Computer Organization and Design" by David A. Patterson and John L. Hennessy**

This book provides a deep dive into **computer architecture**, including instruction set design, memory hierarchy, and parallelism.
3. **"Programming from the Ground Up" by Jonathan Bartlett**
This book introduces **assembly language** programming from scratch and emphasizes how assembly code interfaces with hardware.
4. **"Quantum Computation and Quantum Information" by Michael A. Nielsen and Isaac L. Chuang**
A comprehensive resource on **quantum computing** that covers everything from basic principles to advanced quantum algorithms.

2.2 ONLINE COURSES AND TUTORIALS

1. **MIT OpenCourseWare**
MIT offers free access to courses on computer science, systems programming, computer architecture, and quantum computing. Look for courses like **6.004: Computation Structures** and **6.837: Introduction to Computer Graphics and Imaging**.
2. **Coursera**
Coursera offers various courses in **system programming**, **quantum computing**, and **advanced algorithms**. Courses like **"Introduction to Computer Science"** and **"Quantum Computing Fundamentals"** can help you further explore these topics.
3. **edX**
edX offers in-depth courses from universities like Harvard and MIT. You can explore topics like **systems architecture**, **embedded systems**, and **machine learning**.

2.3 FORUMS AND COMMUNITIES

1. **Stack Overflow**
Stack Overflow is an invaluable resource for troubleshooting

and solving low-level programming issues. The community is vast, and you can find answers to a variety of assembly language and system architecture questions.

2. **Reddit**
Subreddits like **r/learnprogramming**, **r/QuantumComputing**, and **r/embedded** are great places to stay up-to-date with new trends and ask questions related to system architecture and programming.

3. **GitHub**
GitHub hosts a wide variety of **open-source projects**. Explore repositories related to low-level programming, hardware control, and quantum computing to collaborate with other developers and see real-world implementations.

2.4 TOOLS AND SOFTWARE

1. **GDB (GNU Debugger)**
GDB is an essential tool for debugging **assembly programs**. Understanding GDB's features and advanced debugging techniques will allow you to troubleshoot low-level code effectively.

2. **Qiskit**
Qiskit is an open-source quantum computing software development framework provided by IBM. It's a great resource for exploring quantum algorithms and learning quantum programming.

3. **IDA Pro**
IDA Pro is one of the best tools for disassembling and debugging machine code. If you're interested in low-level security analysis or reverse engineering, IDA Pro is an indispensable tool.

3. How to Apply These Skills in Real-World Projects

Now that you've learned the essential principles of **system architecture**, **low-level programming**, and **hardware/software integration**, it's time to apply these skills in real-world projects. Here are some ways you can use your newfound knowledge in practice:

3.1 DEVELOP EMBEDDED SYSTEMS

Embedded systems often require low-level programming, especially when working with **real-time** or **resource-constrained** devices. You can design and implement your own embedded systems projects, such as:

- **IoT Devices**: Build smart devices like sensors, controllers, or even home automation systems.
- **Embedded Control Systems**: Develop systems for controlling industrial equipment, robotics, or medical devices.

3.2 CONTRIBUTE TO OPEN SOURCE PROJECTS

There are numerous open-source projects that require low-level programming expertise. Contributing to these projects can help you gain practical experience and improve your skills. Consider contributing to projects in areas like:

- **Operating System Development**
- **Driver Development** for custom hardware
- **Quantum Computing Libraries** or simulators

3.3 Work on Performance Optimization

Performance-critical applications—like **high-frequency trading systems, real-time gaming engines**, or **video compression algorithms**—require deep system-level optimizations. Use your knowledge of low-level programming to:

- Profile software and identify bottlenecks
- Write assembly routines to optimize performance-critical code
- Experiment with hardware acceleration techniques using **GPUs** or **FPGAs**

3.4 Experiment with Quantum Computing

As **quantum computing** becomes more mainstream, there will be a demand for skilled developers who understand both quantum programming and classical systems. You can explore:

- **Quantum algorithms** like **Shor's algorithm** for factoring or **Grover's algorithm** for searching
- **Quantum-classical hybrid systems,** where quantum computers assist classical systems with complex calculations

3.5 Build Real-Time and Embedded Software

The demand for **real-time systems** and **embedded software** is growing rapidly, especially in industries like automotive (e.g., self-driving cars), healthcare (e.g., medical devices), and aerospace (e.g., flight control systems). These systems often require programming in **assembly language** for **timing accuracy** and **hardware efficiency**.

4. Final Project: Design Your Own System Architecture Project from Scratch

Now that you've learned the fundamental concepts of system architecture, low-level programming, and hardware/software integration, it's time to apply everything you've learned. For your **final project**, you will design a complete system architecture project from scratch. This could involve:

1. **Building an Embedded System**: Design a system that interacts with real-world hardware (e.g., a smart sensor system, a robotic arm, or a wearable device).
2. **Optimizing a High-Performance Application**: Take a **high-level application** and optimize it for performance using low-level programming, assembly language, and hardware acceleration.
3. **Developing a Quantum-Classical Hybrid System**: Combine quantum and classical computing for a real-world use case, like optimization problems or cryptography.

5. Conclusion

Congratulations on completing this book! You now have a solid foundation in **system architecture, low-level programming**, and the integration of **hardware and software**. By applying what you've learned in real-world projects, you'll be able to tackle complex challenges in embedded systems, performance optimization, and even quantum computing. The skills you've gained in this book will serve as a springboard for a successful career in system architecture, enabling you to design efficient, high-performance systems for a wide range of applications.

Remember, the world of **system architecture** is vast and ever-changing, so keep exploring, experimenting, and learning. The future of computing is bright, and with the skills you've developed, you are well-prepared to contribute to the next wave of technological advancements.

www.ingramcontent.com/pod-product-compliance
Lightning Source LLC
LaVergne TN
LVHW022346060326
832902LV00022B/4269